The

Matheny
Manifesto

The

Matheny Manifesto

A YOUNG MANAGER'S OLD-SCHOOL VIEWS
ON SUCCESS IN SPORTS AND LIFE

MIKE MATHENY
with Jerry B. Jenkins

CROWN
ARCHETYPE
NEW YORK

Published in the United States by Crown Archetype, an imprint
of the Crown Publishing Group, a division of Random House LLC,
a Penguin Random House Company, New York.
www.crownpublishing.com

Crown Archetype and colophon is a registered trademark of
Random House LLC.

Library of Congress Cataloging-in-Publication Data
Matheny, Mike, 1970-
   The Matheny Manifesto : a young manager's old school views on
success in sports and life / Mike Matheny with Jerry Jenkins. — First
Edition.
      pages cm
   ISBN 978-0-553-44669-2
   1. Matheny, Mike, 1970- 2. Baseball managers—United States—
Biography. 3. Athletes—United States—Conduct of life. I. Jenkins,
Jerry B. II. Title.
   GV865.M326A3 2015
   796.357092—dc23
   [B]

                                                        2014041741

   ISBN 978-0-553-44669-2
   eBook ISBN 978-0-553-44671-5

PRINTED IN THE UNITED STATES OF AMERICA

Book design by Anna Thompson
Jacket photograph by Rob Tringali/Contributor/Getty Images

10 9 8 7

First Edition

To the greatest influences on my life, my parents:
Jerry and Judy Matheny
Thank you for your humility and wisdom,
for the right word at the right time,
and for silence when it was appropriate
so I could grow on my own.

And to Kristin and the kids:
Tate, Katie, Luke, Jake, and Blaise
You bless me beyond my ability to express.
Thank you for your love and support—no matter what.

ACKNOWLEDGMENTS

Thanks to the coaches who taught me more than just the sport: Ron Golden, Dave Starling, Bill Freehan, Bob Humphreys, Tim Ireland, Chris Bando, Phil Garner, Dave Ricketts, Dave McKay, Dave Duncan, and Tony La Russa.

May I be a responsible vessel to pass along both the baseball and the life lessons.

Special thanks to a coach I never had the honor of meeting but whose thoughts and ideas impacted me more than anyone's. If this book causes even one aspiring coach to research the teachings of John Wooden, the greatest coach in the history of collegiate sports, I will consider the project a success.

I am indebted for life to my personal board, amazed at your willingness to serve so selflessly.

Finally, "Thanks be to God for His indescribable gift!" (2 Corinthians 9:15) I can't say it better than that.

Contents

The Letter That Went Viral

No professional athlete wants to face the end of his career, but it's twice as hard when you're in the prime of life from the neck down. By the close of the 2006 season, I had spent thirteen years behind the plate in big-league baseball and was still, remarkably, in one piece. No one in the game takes the abuse a catcher does, yet at thirty-five I believed I still had a few more seasons in me.

The problem was, I hadn't had an at bat or caught a ball since the last day of May. I had suffered what many of my counterparts in pro football have—a concussion so severe it affected my vision, my ability to think straight, even my ability to engage in normal conversation.

Of all things, it appeared to have been caused by a foul tip to the face mask. But that had to have been only the last straw. Such a shot can ring your bell, even several times a game, but no one had ever heard of one causing real damage. I knew better. Over the years I had endured too many violent collisions at home plate, slamming the back of my head to the ground, rattling my brain.

What followed were the worst eighteen months of my life, as I endured batteries of tests and the fear of never recovering, and before spring training of '07, I had to face that my playing career was over. As I slowly returned to health, I helped out with one of my son's school teams, served as a roving instructor for the St. Louis Cardinals, involved myself in some business ventures, and got on with life, trying to figure out what my future held.

In 2008, some local parents approached me about coaching their youth baseball team the following spring. My own ten-year-old would be on that team, and as a product of youth baseball myself, I found that the more I considered it the stronger I felt about it.

Letting go of major-league baseball was not easy, and I needed something like this while preparing for normal life. I had been raised old school in a small midwestern town, taught to do the right thing because it was the right thing, to never take short-cuts, to be disciplined and selfless and humble. My wife, Kristin, and I were trying to raise our five kids that way, and frankly, we weren't seeing too many other young people with those kinds of values.

Resolve began to grow in me. If I was going to do this, there would be only one way to go about it: all or nothing. This wouldn't be a hobby, a diversion, just your typical local youth baseball team. We'd do it right.

But what if that wasn't what the other parents had in mind? Maybe they just wanted a former big leaguer in the dugout. It was only fair that I spell it out so there'd be no surprises. If they just wanted a coach who knew the game, that was fair. There were plenty to choose from, and I was happy to be just a parent.

But if they wanted a guy who saw this as an opportunity to build character in young men—admittedly very young men—

and teach them life lessons far beyond baseball skills, well, then we could talk.

Frankly, I worried that all they wanted was an elite traveling team with cool equipment and a reputation for winning. The last thing I needed was to hear from every parent who thought his kid ought to be pitching or hitting third or whatever.

I knew I had better clarify things up front for my sake and for theirs. They deserved the chance to withdraw their invitation for me to be the coach before they finalized a decision they would regret.

So on a flight home from New Jersey one night after a guest appearance on the Major League Baseball Network, I pulled out my laptop and wrote them a letter. I didn't call it a manifesto, let alone *my* manifesto. That label didn't come until later, when it somehow found its way to the Internet and went viral, and someone got the idea that *Matheny* and *manifesto* had a ring to it. It has since taken on a life of its own, to my great surprise, but really, the genesis of it was just that I wanted to be clear with the other parents. I wasn't a know-it-all and sure didn't feel I had all the answers. I just didn't want to waste anybody's time.

The letter came to about five single-spaced pages (I didn't hold anything back), and the first person I shared it with was my former big-league teammate John Mabry, who would also have a son on the team and be my assistant coach—that is, if anybody still wanted me after this. John immediately told me, in very colorful language, that though he agreed with my views, if I dared read it to the other parents, I was not to associate his name with it in any way.

Blame it on my concussion, but while I left John out of it, I plunged ahead.

A few nights later, Kristin and I invited the other parents to our home, and after some refreshments and pleasantries, I asked them to gather in front of the fireplace so I could share a few thoughts. I got a quick read of how things were going over once I got started.

Suffice it to say, what became known as the Matheny Manifesto began as the proverbial lead balloon. My voice was the only sound in a cozy family room otherwise silent and still as a mausoleum:

Dear Fellow Parents:

I've always said I would coach only a team of orphans. Why? Because the biggest problem in youth sports is the parents.

But here we are, so it's best I nip this in the bud. If I'm going to do this, I'm asking you to grab the concept that this is going to be ALL about the boys. If anything in this is about you, we need a change of plans.

My main goals are to:

1. teach these boys how to play baseball the right way

2. make a positive impact on them as young men

3. do all this with class

We may not win every game, but we will be the classiest coaches, players, and parents at every game we play. The boys are going to show respect for their teammates, for the opposition, and for the umpires—no matter what.

That being said, you need to know where I stand. I have no hidden agenda, no ulterior motives. My priorities in life will permeate how I coach and what I expect from the boys. My Christian faith guides my life, and while I have never been one to force it down someone's throat, I also think it's cowardly and hypocritical to shy away from what I believe. You parents need to know that when the opportunity presents itself, I will be honest about what I believe. That may make some uncomfortable, but I did that as a player, and I want it out in the open from the beginning that I plan to continue it now.

I believe the biggest role a parent can play is to be a silent source of encouragement. If you ask most boys what they want their parents to do during a game, they'll say, "Nothing." Again, this is ALL about the boys. I know youth league parents feel they must cheer and shout, "Come on, let's go, you can do it!" but even that just adds more pressure.

I will be putting plenty of pressure on these boys to play the game the right way—with class and respect—and they will put too much pressure on themselves and each other as it is. You need to be the silent, constant, source of support.

Let me go on record right now that we will not have good umpiring. The sooner we all understand and accept that, the better off we will be. Pitches that bounce in the dirt will sometimes be called strikes, as will pitches that sail over our heads. Likewise, pitches our guys throw right down the middle will sometimes be called balls.

But at no time will our boys be allowed to show any emotion whatsoever toward the umpire. No shaking their heads, no pouting, no saying anything. That is my job, and I will do it well. I once got paid to handle those guys, and I will let them know when they need to hear something.

Really, I'm doing you a favor you probably don't realize at this point. I have eliminated a lot of work for you. All you have to do is get your son there on time, and enjoy. And all they need to hear from you is that you enjoyed watching them and that you hope they had fun.

I know it's going to be very hard not to coach from the stands and yell encouraging things, but trust me on this: coaching and yelling (even encouraging) works against their development and enjoyment. I'm not saying you can't clap for them when they do well. I'm saying that if you entrust your child to me to coach him, then let me do that job.

That doesn't change the fact that a large part of how much your child improves *is* your responsibility. What makes a difference for kids at this level is how much repetition they get, and that goes for pitching, hitting, and fielding. You can help out tremendously by playing catch, throwing batting practice, hitting ground balls, or finding an instructor who will do this in your place. The more of this your child can get, the better. The one constant I've found with major leaguers is that someone spent a lot of time with them between games.

I am completely fine with your son getting lessons from whomever you see fit. The only problem I will have is if you or your instructor counters what I'm teaching the team. I won't teach a lot of mechanics at first, but I will teach a mental approach, and I'll expect the boys to comply. If I see your son doing something drastically wrong mechanically, I will talk with you or his instructor and clear it up.

The same will hold true with pitching coaches. We will have a pitching philosophy, and will teach pitchers and catchers how to call a game and why we choose the pitches we choose. There'll be no guessing; we'll have reasons for the pitches we throw. A pitching coach will be helpful for the boys to get their arms in shape and be ready to throw when spring arrives. Every boy on this team will be worked as a pitcher. We will not overuse these young arms and will keep a close watch on the number of innings each boy is pitching.

I will be throwing so much info at these boys that they will suffer from overload for a while, but eventually they'll get it. I'm a stickler about the thought process of the game. I'll talk nonstop about situational hitting, situational pitching, and defensive preparation. The question they'll hear most is "What were you thinking?"

What were you thinking when you threw that pitch?

What were you thinking during that at bat?

What were you thinking before the pitch was thrown; what were you anticipating?

I am a firm believer that this game is more mental than physical, and though the mental aspect may be more difficult, it can be learned by ten- and eleven-year-olds.

If it sounds like I'm going to be demanding, you're exactly right. I'm definitely going to demand their attention, and I'm going to require effort.

Attitude, concentration, and effort are three things they can control. If they give me those three things every time they show up, they will have a great experience.

It works best for all of us if you would plan on turning

your kid over to me and the assistant coaches when you drop him off and entrust him to us for the two hours or so that we have scheduled for a game or practice. I want him to take responsibility for his own water, not have you running to the concession stand or standing behind the dugout asking if he's thirsty or hungry or hot—and I'd appreciate if you would share this information with other guests, like grandparents.

If there is an injury, obviously we'll call you, but otherwise let's pretend he's at work for a short time and that you've been granted the privilege of watching. I want them at games early so we can stretch and loosen up, and I will have a meeting with just the boys after the game. After that, they are all yours again.

As I'm writing this I realize I sound like a kids-baseball dictator, but I really believe this will make things easier for everyone involved.

[And as I was reading this, believe me, I knew it was coming across even stronger than when I had been writing it. In my peripheral vision, I could tell mouths were hanging open. I began seriously considering what else I could do with my spare time that summer.]

Now let me be clear about family priorities. I'm a firm believer that the family is the most important institution in the lives of these guys. Family events are much more important than the sports events. I just ask that you show consideration to the rest of the team and let the team manager and me know when your son will miss practice or a game, and let us know as soon as possible. There will be times when *I* have to miss for family reasons or other commitments.

So, if your son misses a game or a practice, it's not the end of the world, but out of respect for the kids that *have* made it, he may be asked to run, have his playing time altered a bit, or even be moved down in the batting order.

Along with where he hits in the lineup and his amount of playing time, which position a kid plays is one of the most complained-about issues. I need you to know that I am trying to develop each boy individually, and I will give him a chance to learn and play any position he is interested in. I will have each tell me his favorite position and what other position he would like to learn about.

I believe this team will eventually be competitive. When we get to where we are focusing on winning, like in a tournament, for example, we are going to put the boys in the positions that will give us the best opportunity. Meanwhile, as the season progresses, there's a chance your son may be playing a position he doesn't like. That's when I most need your support about his role on the team.

I know times have changed, but one of the greatest lessons my father taught me was that my coach was always right—even when he was wrong. That principle is a great life lesson about how things really work. Our culture has lost respect for authority, because kids hear their parents complain about teachers and coaches. That said, I'm determined to exhibit enough humility to come to your son and apologize if I've treated him wrong. Meanwhile, give me the benefit of the doubt that I have his best interests in mind, even if you're convinced I'm wrong.

I need you to know that we are most likely going to lose many games this year. The main reason is that we need to find out how we measure up against the local talent pool, and the only way to know that is to play against some of the best teams. I'm convinced that if the boys put their work in at home and give me their best effort, we'll be able to play with just about any team. Time will tell.

I also believe there is enough local talent that we will not have to do a large amount of travel, if any. That may be disappointing for you whose sons play only baseball and who look forward to the out-of-town experiences. But I also know this will be a relief for parents who have traveled throughout the United States and Canada for hockey and soccer looking for better competition. In my experience, we have traveled all over the Midwest and have found just as good competition right in our backyard. If this season goes well, we will entertain the idea of travel in the future.

The boys will be required to show up ready to play every time they come to the field. That means shirts tucked in, hats on straight, and no pants drooping to their knees.

There is never an excuse for lack of hustle on a baseball field. From the first step outside the dugout they will hustle. They will quickly jog to their positions, to the plate, and back to the bench after an out. We will run out every hit harder than any team we play, and we will learn to always back up our teammates. Every single play, every player will be required to move to a spot. Players who don't hustle and run out balls will not play. The boys will catch on to this quickly.

Baseball becomes very boring when players are not thinking about the next play and what they could possibly do to help the team. Players on the bench will not be messing around. I will constantly talk with them about situations and what they would do in a specific position or if they were the batter. There is as much to learn on the bench as there is on the field.

All this will take time for the boys to conform to. They are kids, and I am not trying to take away from that, but I believe they can bear down and concentrate during games and practices.

I know this works because it was how I was taught the game and how our parents acted in the stands. We started our Little League team when I was ten years old in a little suburb of Columbus, Ohio. We had a very disciplined coach who expected the same from us. We committed eight summers to this man, and we were rewarded for our efforts. I went to Michigan, one teammate went to Miami of Florida, one to Ohio State, two to North Carolina, one to Central Florida, two to Kent State, and most of the others played smaller Division 1 or Division 2 baseball. Five of us went on to play professionally—not a bad showing from a small-town team.

I'm not guaranteeing this is what's going to happen to our boys, but I want you to see that this system works. I know that by now you're asking if this is what you want to get yourself into, and I understand that for some it may not be the right fit. But I also think there's a great opportunity here for these boys to grow together and learn lessons that will last far beyond their baseball experience.

Let me know as soon as possible whether or not this is a commitment that you and your son want to make.

Thanks.

—Mike

I finally looked up into the eyes of a bunch of parents who had been every bit as successful as I had, and in many cases more so. A lot of them looked away. They loved their children the way Kristin and I loved ours, and I had just told them—right up front—that parents were what was wrong with youth sports. They had to be thinking, *He may know how to play baseball, but who made him the guru of how to fix society?*

Who wants to be told they're doing something wrong, especially when it comes to their kids? For all I knew, they would take me up on my offer to forget this whole idea, and I would be the one in the stands who had dropped his kid off to play ball.

But after several agonizing seconds, one of the fathers surprised me by saying, "Well, I'm in."

They gave me the chance, and I put into practice what I believed was right. It wasn't always easy, and not everyone was on board from the beginning. Not everyone lasted. But good values are good values for a reason, and in the end, they work.

In this book I want to talk about the lessons we taught and the many we learned in the process, some painful but all valuable. I'll tell a lot of stories along the way, from my childhood and upbringing, my days as a young ballplayer, a college player, a minor leaguer, and a big leaguer (as both a player and a manager).

I want to tell you how I arrived at the philosophy I espouse today, and I also want to assure you that I in no way claim it originated with me. Its values are as old as the Bible, and it's entirely opposite of the me-first youth culture the media tries to sell our kids twenty-four hours a day on screens as small as their pockets and as big as their bedroom walls.

But if there's one thing I've learned, it's that nothing worth doing right is easy.

In telling the story of how the team came together, grew slowly, learned from failure, and eventually developed into winners athletically and in character, I also want to examine how these values apply to life beyond baseball, beyond sports, and can plant a seed of hope in the next generation. While I have coached only boys and now men, and will refer to them frequently in this book, I want to add that everything here also applies to girls and women. My wife was a college field hockey player, and my daughter is a college ice hockey player. We all have much to learn.

Only a minuscule fraction of the boys and girls you and I coach will ever make a living or even put themselves through college as athletes. But they can all become better men and women if we can instill in them values they can apply in the workplace, in their homes and families, and in their communities.

What could be more worthwhile than that?

— PART I —

The Problem

1

Whatever Happened to the Love of the Game?

I'm a fierce competitor, and I don't apologize for that. I want only that kind of player on my teams, too. But while coaching—and parenting—in youth sports, I have to keep that in its proper perspective. To create an atmosphere in which young people can reach their full potential, I must first make sure they develop a love and a passion for their sport, before any other lessons can be taught—including the will to win. Argue with me all you want, but I'm going from what I'm hearing from my current players, former coaches, and former teammates.

When I was a kid, we loved sports. We played baseball, basketball, and football because they were fun and we enjoyed them. Organized sports were great, but most of the time we played on our own. Hall of Fame pitcher Nolan Ryan has said that the difference between the way kids play today and the way he and his friends played is that now they only play with uniforms on.

Somehow, the more organized sports became, the more they became about the parents and not about the kids. All of a sudden, kids didn't seem to love sports as much as I did when I was their age—and that's something I thought needed to change.

MY VERY FIRST baseball memory was Wiffle ball in the backyard, baseball in its purest form. I was the third of four boys growing up in Reynoldsburg, Ohio, a suburb of Columbus. We played all sports, competed at everything, and like everyone else— probably including you—made up our own rules.

Mom tried to change those rules. She wanted to make every ball we hit over the fence a three-out infraction, since the neighbors always complained about us being in their yard. But what kid could ever follow that rule? Baseball is all about home runs and mimicking your favorite player, and in those days I was Tom Seaver when I pitched and Johnny Bench when I was at the plate.

Sometimes I would work on my left-handed swing so I could watch the ball bounce off the neighbors' roof. My brothers and I would make sure Mom wasn't watching before we hopped the fence to retrieve the only ball we had that wasn't cracked.

Even though we aimed away from the house with the dog, that animal had a sporting goods store's worth of our Wiffle balls. *The Sandlot* movie, which would come along a couple of years after I signed a pro contract, could have been our story. But none of us dared go to the door or jump that fence.

We talked our dad into putting up lights so that we could play at night, and often we played so late the neighbors yelled out their window that it was time for the game to be over.

It seemed my older brother Rusty could throw a Wiffle ball

ninety miles an hour. He loved putting welts on my bare back, since pegging—throwing the runner out between bases by nailing him with the ball—was permitted. Mom tried to change that rule, too, to no avail.

I don't know what your game looked like, but here are some more of our details:

- Rock, paper, scissors served as our review process.
- The tie always went to the runner.
- Appropriating Dad's black electrical tape to give the skinny yellow bat a little more weight was deemed completely legal.
- The greatest accessory was a plastic helmet from your favorite team.
- A drive into the far corner of the yard was an easy double if you hustled out of the box.
- Second base was a Frisbee we hadn't tossed for years.
- A worn patch of dirt served as home plate.

I fell in love with the game of baseball in that backyard before I ever wore a jersey or played on an official team. I learned base running, cutoffs and relays, rundowns, even bench-clearing brawls with my brothers and neighborhood kids.

My dad worked construction and my mom for a church missionary association, so there was never enough money for an Atari, Nintendo, or Xbox. I'm grateful, because if we'd had those, I might never have known what baseball was really all about.

We kept score but never remembered, dinner was an annoyance, and the end of summer was a tragedy.

One of the first things I did for my own kids was build them a Wiffle ball field on our property—backstop, bases, home-run fence, scoreboard, lights, sprinkler system, the whole bit. On their birthdays, our kids get to choose what we do, and almost without fail, even to this day, it includes Wiffle ball late into the night—sometimes until dawn. Big-league teams have played Wiffle ball at our place.

What I love about baseball has evolved over the years, though.

As a first-time player on an organized team, I loved a chocolate swirl ice cream cone with sprinkles at Dairy Queen after the game, even when we lost.

I later fell in love with playing in front of a crowd and the thrill of making a play.

Back then, fun trumped winning, and wearing the same jersey as your friends was the definition of success.

I loved the smell of the bubble gum you could get only at the ball field, and seeing how many pieces I could keep in my mouth during the game.

Over time and the onset of puberty, fun turned to ferocity, and testosterone made every game live or die. I learned how much it really meant to me when I couldn't control the tears after letting a ball roll through my legs cost my team the game.

I soon realized the sport had changed for me. Far beyond a source of joy and a sense of accomplishment, it came to define my social status. Baseball became part of who I was—not just how others saw me, but how I viewed myself. Its heroes, past and present, became like Greek gods, and getting even a glimpse of them in person was surreal.

I'll never forget getting to travel and seeing how I matched up to the talent in other areas, finding out how much more work I had to do. How exciting, that first out-of-town trip without my family, my first night in a hotel with a bunch of kids too rowdy to sleep—or let anyone else for that matter.

I loved using a hose to fill my jug that needed to last an entire day, showing up early to rake the infield, praying it wouldn't rain, enjoying a Snickers bar as a between-games meal, and being covered with dirt from head to toe.

Who can forget discovering you're on the local scouts' radar and have a legitimate chance to play a game that can pay for your education, are you kidding me? What's not to love about showing up on a college campus and joining a team of guys you've never met but you know already have your back?

Why did I come to love baseball?

The game became the pacesetter for my life. What could top any of these:

Lying in bed at the University of Michigan, dreaming of playing professionally, earning a degree along the way because you can catch and throw.

Getting an actual check for signing your name, just because you have potential.

Waking up every day knowing you have a chance to improve your odds of making it to the Show, and realizing you actually play *every single day.*

Now occasionally praying *for* rain so your body can recoup.

Getting the call that tells you your lifelong dream has come true and you've become one of the select few who ever make it.

Sharing a locker room with superstars and future Hall of Famers and finding yourself in the same lineup.

Getting paid to play a game—well enough to get a great start in life.

Asking for autographs from legends, and having them actually engage you in conversation as if you're in the same fraternity—because you are.

Truly realizing the depth of your love for the game by how you feel when it's taken from you—twice.

Getting another chance to chase the dream and actually experience a winning season.

Feeling the buzz of the crowd in the postseason and the month-long celebration known as October baseball.

Stepping up to the plate in the World Series and facing the best of the best on the baseball world's biggest stage.

Having hung in there long enough for your kids to get to walk onto a major-league field and understand the passion the fans hold for this great game and its players.

And finally to watch the sun set on a career some believed would never happen, and to humbly, silently say, "I told you I could."

MAYBE MY WIFE, Kristin, and John and Ann Mabry were the only three parents who could truly understand where I was coming from that night, a true lover of baseball standing before them and reading what otherwise had to sound like a very strange letter. I was no guru, hardly a know-it-all, and I certainly didn't want to come across as a Little League dictator.

But neither did I have any interest in being involved in a youth baseball program that disgraced the game that had virtually been my life and helped shape my character. Ironically, if I had learned anything from baseball, from all the coaching and the training and the practices and the development, it was that so much more went into making a child an adult than teaching athletic skills and how to win games.

In the few short decades since my childhood, I had seen a shocking shift in the values and actions of parents and coaches that I believed made it nearly impossible for the youth of today to love the game the way I do. If I was right, youth sports was long overdue for an overhaul of business as usual.

2

The Problem with New-School Parents

Matt Lauer, interviewing Meryl Streep on the *Today* show, tells her he heard she was a soccer mom. "I'm trying to picture you on the sidelines in the stands. Did you ever say or do anything at a game that your kids were playing in that would make all those Oscars blush?"

Streep says, "I was not allowed to make a sound at a game—ever!"

Somebody in the Streep household got it right.

I never imagined that within a couple of years I would become manager of the St. Louis Cardinals and find that almost overnight I could be heard on a much larger platform than I ever dreamed. My top priority has become the success of that organization and my players, of course, but I'm still passionate about this issue of youth sports and take seriously what I believe is my responsibility to speak out. You never know how long you're going to have such an opportunity, and I don't want to waste it.

Immediately a whole new audience was watching and listening to what the "young," the "untested," the "surprise choice"—believe me, I heard them all—new skipper of the Cardinals would say and do after being handed the reins of the defending World Series champions from the legendary Tony La Russa.

I'll get to all the details of how that miracle happened—yes, in many ways I do think it was a God thing—but in the midst of all that controversy, the press discovered I had a "cause," and it struck a nerve. The letter to parents had already gone viral and become known as The Matheny Manifesto, but if people hadn't been aware of it by then, they were now. The press used it as a hook in their stories about me.

I began hearing from people everywhere I went—parents, coaches, former teammates, broadcasters, you name it—that the letter had resonated with them. Some told me they had been raised the way I had and wanted to see a return to those values. Others told me horror stories of what had become of their once proud youth-league teams. Still others said their league made all its coaches read the letter at the start of the season.

I was encouraged. Our initial team, which I called the Wolverines in honor of my alma mater, Michigan, had started with just those silk-screened T-shirts and broke a lot of rules. The parents agreed to let the coaches coach and to fight their instincts and sit on their hands in the stands. It wasn't easy, but most of them did it.

Some didn't. Some couldn't. Some had to go. There were those who had to be dismissed. Others were happy to leave a program where we put less emphasis on winning, refused to dominate other teams, and purposely moved players around in what appeared to be nonsensical lineups. Plus, we didn't travel far, didn't allow swaggering, and insisted on good sportsmanship and class.

Except for those who left, plenty of people were impressed.

Hillerich & Bradsby, the makers of Louisville Slugger bats, liked what they saw and became our sponsor, and we changed our name to the TPX Warriors—*TPX* being one of their brand names and *Warriors* having a better ring to it, I thought, than *Wolverines*. Soon we were inundated with people wanting their kids to play at different age levels, so we branched out and added tryouts for more teams.

At the first tryout, one dad showed up and seemed to do and say all the right things. But the very next day he began bothering the coaches, and when one asked him to please let the staff handle the process, he argued and then complained to other parents. When I asked him to leave he accused us of being cliquish and tried to talk people out of participating. But by then we had already established a good reputation, and he never gained any traction. The fact is, when you try to do something right, you're always going to have those for whom it's just not a good fit.

We've learned to just face it head-on, and for us it's not that big a deal anymore. It's usually more of a blow to the parents' pride than the kid's. We say, "If it's not the perfect fit, why waste your time? If our structure or our style is causing issues, whether at home or within your family, or you're having second thoughts about why you got into this—if anything about it is less than positive, go find positive. We'll help you find your best scenario. It's youth sports."

I had been clear I didn't want conversations with parents about where their kid plays or bats in the order, but sure enough I took a call from a mother who wanted to know why her son wasn't batting in a certain spot in the order on one of the teams.

I said, "Let me stop you there. You know that coach is doing what he thinks is best for everybody. No one is batting in one particular spot yet, and—"

"I know," she said. "But can't he just keep moving everyone else around and leave him—"

"You realize what you've just done, right?"

"Excuse me?" she said.

"Just so you know, you're going where we said we weren't going to go. This is not what you agreed to when you signed the agreement."

I gave her a little explanation about how to help her son improve and hoped that was the end of it, but a few days later I got another call. She said, "I still think the coach should—"

"I hate to do this," I said, "because we love your son and he's a good player, but you've just cost him his spot on the team."

After a long silence, she said, "You're serious."

"One hundred percent. This is how it has to go. You agreed to this."

She said, "I'm going to be in big trouble here. My husband's not gonna forgive me for this, because he loves him being on that team."

Those are difficult conversations, but hard decisions have to be made. Otherwise, a program built on honesty and character becomes a sham.

In that case the boy was the victim of an overzealous parent, but he jumped right into something else. We always tried to help families find another team or league that might better fit their needs.

PEOPLE WERE EAGER to have their kids playing with us, and eventually we grew to seven teams. Clearly we were onto something that was working. So why was I conflicted? Because I didn't want to be guilty of the very thing we were trying to avoid: coming off like I thought I had all the answers.

On the other hand, I don't want to sway an inch from my

contention that youth sports are screwed up and parents are to blame. I stand behind that 100 percent, and I can't be wishy-washy about it.

So if you'll bear with me and accept that I see myself as just a fellow traveler on this journey, that I'm just gratified to find that maybe we've stumbled onto something that can make a real difference in people's lives, let me explain what I see as the root of the problem and how we might attack it.

Watching their kids play sports becomes many parents' primary activity. Other parents become their main social group and their entire identity begins to revolve around their kids. All of a sudden, whether or not their kid makes the team can become almost as important as whether Dad or Mom keeps their job.

Also, a discerning observer can see a great player on the field and quickly determine—from body language alone—who his parents are in the stands. It's great to be proud of your kids, but it can be dangerous when that pride comes to define you as a person. If you're cheerful and upbeat when he's doing well but despondent and grumpy when he's not, beware. If you treat him great when he succeeds but act as if he has let you down when he's failed, don't be surprised when he decides, "I'm done, I'm out. You treat me better when I'm not playing sports."

This happens at every level, by the way, and not just with parents. I've seen it in the major leagues between managers and players. Superstars naturally get preferential treatment, and maybe they deserve it. What hurts is when an everyday, journeyman player goes on a hot streak or even has an all-star half-season. Suddenly he's looked at in a different light. Maybe he has developed a fan club or a cheering section, the press has taken a liking to him, even a commercial or two or an endorsement deal has landed in his lap.

Now, for a time, it seems everyone wants a piece of him. His manager has a bag of souvenirs he'd like signed for his kids and/ or grandkids, and he even consults the player during crucial game situations.

Then comes the inevitable slump, or the player just settles back into his realistic performance level. He's still a quality ball-player, still a big leaguer, still a professional. But because he's not the standout he was last week or last month, he doesn't get the same attention from anyone anymore, including his manager.

Manager, boss, parent—whoever treats a player, a subordinate, or a kid that way is exhibiting a simple, shallow character trait: conditional love. And I don't know one recipient of it who can't see right through it.

I've seen parents who can hardly talk to their kids when they come off the field if they've had a bad game. What kid is going to put up with that for long?

Then there are those parents who just flat ought to be ashamed of themselves. I'll never forget one of my sons' very first orga-nized ice hockey games. This was in the off-season during my years playing with the Cardinals. Playing baseball for more than half the year took me away from so many normal family activi-ties, I was really looking forward to getting the chance to just be a normal dad.

Usually if I got to watch one of the kids play a sport, I would try to sit in a secluded spot where I wouldn't be recognized and just try to enjoy the game. Since this was at a hockey rink with a bunch of parents bundled up in parkas, Kristin and I sat with the crowd, chuckling at the little guys wearing their bulky hockey gear for the first time and struggling to stay upright on the ice.

The game had hardly begun when it became clear that the kids could barely move, let alone skate. I was trying to keep an eye on my own son, but there was one kid who looked about twice the size of anyone else out there and another who looked that much smaller than everyone else. Once he got going, the big boy didn't know how to stop. He'd plow into anyone in his way until he slammed into the boards. It was clear he meant no harm. Like the rest of the kids, he just had no clue.

When this happened more than once, a father behind me screamed something, and I figured he was calling to somebody on the ice. Then a burly guy in front of me turned and said something back to him, and the next thing I knew these two were going at it and I was trying to keep the big one out of my lap. I noticed the screamer behind me was a little guy, but he called the other one out and asked him if he wanted to settle it outside!

I thought surely the other parents would talk these two idiots out of doing something so stupid, but they all turned back to the game. The big guy wasn't about to back down in front of everybody, so he headed outside with the little guy right behind him.

I followed, determined to talk some sense into them. As soon as we got out the door I grabbed the little one, who was squirming like he was high. I turned to the big guy, who could have dropped the other with one punch and was clearly embarrassed. I said, "Do me a favor and go back inside, man. Nothing good is gonna come of this. If I let go of this guy, you're probably both gonna go to jail."

To his credit, the big guy swallowed his pride and went back in while the little guy cussed him out. As soon as the big guy was out of sight, the little one calmed down and said, "That was some season you guys had, Mike. The Cards gonna be good again next year?"

People. All I could do was shake my head.

That set the tone for hockey. Every game we went to, parents were yelling. They yelled at their own kids. They yelled at the other team. They yelled at the coaches. They yelled at the referees. I wanted nothing to do with all that. I'd get myself a large coffee and find an empty corner where I just sat by myself and tried to enjoy the game the best I could.

Still, there were incidents I couldn't ignore. Once a guy came wandering down and sat in the front row behind the glass so he could yell at the goalie, who must've been his grandson, because this was an older gentleman (and I use that term loosely). He screamed at this kid relentlessly. When the boy appeared not to listen, the man would jump to his feet and scream louder. Once, when the boy appeared to turn his head away, the man leapt from his seat, but when he opened his mouth to scream, his top partial came flying out and hit the glass. He quickly pinned it there and carefully slid it up until he could pop it back in his mouth and sit down.

People.

Think about it, you've got kids doing something voluntarily, something they want to do because they thought they'd enjoy it. They show up, they start to learn, and all they get is grief from the people they care about most in the world. Very rarely do I go to a youth game of any sport where I don't see somebody bawling out a kid. It's no wonder when it comes time to sign up for that sport the following year that the kid doesn't want to subject himself to that again. He'd rather stay home playing video games.

Then you get those parents who rationalize by saying, "If I quit yelling at them, that means I don't care about them anymore."

Meanwhile, the kid is thinking, *Please stop caring.*

I've seen that attitude lead to crazy philosophies and adages like this one: "Never allow your child to quit."

That may sound noble on the surface, but I've never understood it. Great, your child is not a quitter. Nobody wants to raise a quitter, do they? But what happens when they really do need a break from the game? What happens when they've grown to hate it and resent you for making them continue in what they see as an awful situation? Three of my four sons asked to quit baseball at one point or another. Two took a year off and the other came back begging to play again that same season. I shudder to think what would've happened if I had made them keep playing no matter what. My fear is, of course, that they would have soured on the game they now love as much as I do and would have given it up for good—because of me. Imagine.

Naturally, a lot of kids see the yelling as their parents taking their frustration out on them. Regardless how young they are, they know a lack of self-control when they see it. Then, when the kids make errors or strike out or miss a basket or let a soccer goal dribble through and then express *their* anger by throwing equipment or cussing—because everyone else is doing it—*they* get in trouble. They get benched.

Because their hypocritical parents have been bad models.

That was one of the major things I was determined to avoid as the coach of a youth baseball team and why I felt it so important to stress to the other parents. I could have, and probably should have, given those parents the benefit of the doubt. They were bright, well-educated, successful, loving people who wanted the best for their kids. But I wanted this on the table from the beginning. It was going to be about the kids and not about us.

IMAGINE YOURSELF IN the most stressful situation possible, with all your family and friends watching. Imagine being asked to do something so difficult that most people fail three times more often than they succeed. Now imagine that the people you love most in the world are screaming at the top of their lungs at you while you're trying to do this.

Sound tough?

Welcome to the world of youth sports.

I don't know how to explain the difference between how parents act today and how they did when I was a kid. I must have grown up in a cocoon. I played hundreds of games, and there were never parents and coaches screaming like there are now. A lot of it, I think, had to do with the fact that other parents wouldn't have allowed it. Most people simply didn't act like that back then.

I ask everyone in the game, from current players to Hall of Famers, "How did your parents act at your games?" Overwhelmingly, nearly unanimously, they tell me they never heard a word from them. A couple, myself included, would hear a distinct whistle, voice, or clap they recognized when they did something well. But never any screaming or yelling or instructing from their parents during the game. Coincidence that we all had the same kinds of parents? I don't think so.

What struck our team parents most was the idea that we were taking the pressure off them to perform. Many parents felt they needed to show their kid how crazy they were about him by how crazy they went in the stands. But the truth is, it's completely the opposite.

I told the parents in the letter to just clap because—and this is coming from kids—it actually adds more pressure when they hear their parents even yell, "You can do this!" It's *not* encouraging. It actually adds stress! Here's why:

The kid is already under incredible pressure he's put on

himself, standing in that box or standing on that mound. He should be focusing on his teammates and his coaches and the task at hand.

But when, on top of all that, he has this extra so-called encouragement coming from people who are supposed to care, regardless whether he succeeds or not, it's just too much.

The parents, naturally, are trying so hard to help him succeed and think they are boosting his confidence by saying, "You can do this!"

But then what if he doesn't succeed? He's already crushed because he has let down himself and his team and his coaches. But now you, too?

My parents thought I could do it, and I couldn't. Many kids just break and say, "Forget it."

He has the rest of his life to learn about real pressure and disappointment. Let him have fun. You'll be amazed by how much more enjoyable the game will be for you when you take the pressure off yourself to be the world's best cheerleader—and be just a spectator and fan of your child doing something that he loves.

You'll be glad you did. Your child will, too.

3

Coaches with Complexes, or You're Not Billy Martin

It breaks your heart. It is designed to break your heart. The game begins in the spring, when everything else begins again, and it blossoms in the summer, filling the afternoons and evenings, and then as soon as the chill rains come, it stops and leaves you to face the fall alone. You count on it, rely on it to buffer the passage of time, to keep the memory of sunshine and high skies alive, and then just when the days are all twilight, when you need it most, it stops.

FROM *A Great and Glorious Game: Baseball Writings of*
A. Bartlett Giamatti (© 1998 BY A. BARTLETT GIAMATTI)

Bart Giamatti and Billy Martin had two things in common but were otherwise about as different as two men could be. They both loved baseball and died too young—Giamatti at fifty-one and Martin at sixty-one—in the last quarter of 1989.

Giamatti became president of Yale University by the time he was forty and the commissioner of major-league baseball by the time he was fifty. Martin was a scrappy infielder for seven big-league teams and then became one of the most notorious managers in the history of baseball, managing five different teams. He was hired and fired five different times by the Yankees alone.

So why do I mention Giamatti and Martin together?

What lover of baseball wouldn't want to be able to express himself about the game as well as Bart Giamatti did above? I sure would. But I can't, so I just quote that paragraph from his book.

So why do so many amateur baseball coaches think they can be Billy Martin? It's one thing to try to play Billy Ball—with lots of bunting and running and taking the extra base. But so many guys take it a step further. They strut, they posture, they throw their hats, they kick dirt, and they argue with umpires half their age. Worst of all, they play to win at all costs, run up the score, and scream at their players.

Billy Martin did this for a living, and half of what he did was for show. He lived his life on TV, and the fans ate it up. His players could take it. They were paid well, and they were grown men.

Many amateur youth-sports coaches are thrust into their positions and are in over their heads. Others long for the job and believe they were born for it. Don't get me wrong. There are countless wonderful people coaching kids all over the United States. And I plan to share a lot of examples of those with suggestions for how to be a good coach. You'll find few people more sympathetic to the pressures coaches face than a big-league manager, but first let's take a look at what's wrong with too many, specifically those who think they are Billy Martin.

ONE OF MY first coaches as a kid was one who just couldn't keep his eyes off his own son. To protect the innocent, let's call that boy Russell. The whole game, all game, every game, all we heard—all anyone could hear (players, the other team, parents, fans, everybody)—was poor Russell being hollered at by his dad.

It was "Russell, catch the ball! Russell, tag the runner! Russell, move left! Russell, guard the line! Russell, swing! Russell, that ball was too high! Russell! Russell! Russell!"

No surprise, Russell didn't play sports very long.

That's no coincidence.

Even as a kid, I couldn't help but compare that coach with my own father. My dad would put in long hours operating heavy machinery, a tough job that beats you up all day. He'd come home covered with dirt, and you could tell all he wanted to do was get cleaned up and relax. But he would always grab a glove and go play catch with me and my brother or throw batting practice for us. He never turned us down.

I have a friend who likes to say, "It's the pictures," which is his way of complimenting a person whose pictures—whose actions—line up with their words. My dad didn't say a lot, and he still doesn't, but his pictures tell you what he's passionate about. He coached me for a couple of years when I was nine and ten before I joined a traveling team, but Dad also served as my personal coach until I went off to play at the University of Michigan.

When he coached my team, he never played favorites. And when I played for other coaches, he never got in the way.

At home he'd have me do drills in the garage, which we had

turned into a little rec room with a net to keep us boys from doing too much damage. He would have me bounce out from my catcher's stance and get balls after I blocked them. He taught me all he knew, reinforced the basics, and would get creative, too. He was always making up different workouts and contraptions.

Once, as a young teen, I made my own soft-toss machine out of pieces of our backyard fence, my mother's mop bucket, and chicken wire. It worked okay, but when Dad got home I figured I'd be in trouble for the fence, the bucket, or the wire—one of the three. But he was excited that I had been conscientious enough to put it all together, and he helped me build an even better one.

But, again, Dad knew to let my coaches be my coaches.

Now, be honest—or ask someone you can trust to tell you the truth about yourself: Are you one of those coaches more interested in your own kid—promoting them either for temporary success or trying to put them in position so they can fulfill some big dream down the road—than you are in the well-being of your team as a whole?

If, despite all the other things going on in a game, you find yourself hollering your own kid's name most of the time, it's time to look in the mirror and reevaluate yourself as a coach. You might be unable to keep your eyes off your own kid. If that's the case, you need to step aside, because until you can conquer that, a bunch of kids are going to pay the price.

Too many youth coaches are convinced they need a room full of trophies before they can consider themselves successful. Is that what you think youth sports is about, your win-loss record? Hear me. Amateur coaches do not move up the food chain by winning, and measuring yourself that way is a trap that can lead to unbelievable arrogance.

I'm going to suggest something that may sound too simplistic, but humor me. Ask yourself, "Why am I coaching?"

If your answer has anything to do with you, it's time to reconsider your motives. You may need to find someone to take your place. Believe me, I know, coaching youth sports is a thankless job. There's always more grief than joy. But more long-term damage can be done to kids than to you if you're coaching for the wrong reasons.

REMEMBER WHEN RUTGERS University fired its basketball coach in the spring of 2013 after a videotape of his practices was leaked to the media showing him berating his players, firing balls at them, and calling them names? I hesitate to cite that example because it's so extreme, and your first response might be "Well, I may holler a little, but at least I'm not like *him*."

It's easy to point your finger and forget to look in the mirror. But there's something we can all learn from this. How do you coach? What is your style? How do you motivate your players when you lose your cool? More important, as I asked above, *why* do you coach? How you answer that is the key to how you will coach and, ultimately, how and what you communicate. And, as you can imagine, this applies to how you parent, even if you're not a coach, because it shines a light on your motives.

Retired NFL defensive lineman Joe Ehrmann wrote one of my favorite books, *InSideOut Coaching,* in which he explains the difference between a *transactional* and a *transformational* coach.

He describes a *transactional* coach as one who will do or say to his team whatever it takes to win.

A *transformational* coach is one more interested in growing his players beyond their performance.

Ehrmann writes, "If interpersonal expectations, codes of conduct, and a dedication to transformation over transaction are communicated clearly, the positive impact on an athlete's development not only can win a game, it can change a life."

Our role as coaches is not just to build up the scoreboard but also to build up our players so that they become character-filled leaders who will have an impact on those around them. As coaches and as parents, we should set this as our primary goal. When we do, the way we communicate to our players and kids will look very different. Screaming and yelling no longer have a place in our tool kits.

We must find ways to develop our athletes not just as players but also as people. Let's forget pointing the finger at an extreme example and congratulating ourselves because "at least I'm not as bad as he is," and instead seriously reevaluate the way we coach.

For example, let me tell you what I see coaches doing at almost every level. They find that one kid who can get them the win and they start throwing him to the point where they risk injury. It's not fair to him, and it's not fair to other players who'd like to try their hand at pitching. But if the coach is thinking only of his own record, you know the choice he's going to make when the game is on the line.

Then you've got these teams that will jump out to a big lead, and the coach feels they need to just keep running. The poor kid behind the plate for the other team has no chance. He's trying to hurry his pitcher, calling pitches he hopes will help him cut down a runner, but now he's overthrowing, the fielders are chasing the ball all over the field, and the game is getting further and further out of hand.

I mean, really, you want to win, but again, you're not Billy Martin; you're not in the big leagues. You're not being paid millions, and your livelihood is not on the line. You know, even in the majors there are unwritten rules about this stuff. When you start to humiliate the opposition, what purpose does that serve?

Running up the score is not limited to baseball either. I recently had a conversation with two basketball officials, one who refs college games and the other junior high and high school games. I was amazed at how similar their experiences are to the baseball world. They find some coaches teaching their student athletes the game—and how to do the right thing. But they also have nightmare stories of coaches desperately missing the mark.

One team started the second half with a fifty-point lead but still had all five starters in and was running a full-court press. During a time-out the ref asked the head coach if he was really going to keep this up for the rest of the game. The coach said his team needed to stay sharp, and he believed in never holding back. The ref told the coach he was "basketball ignorant, hurting kids on both teams."

Exactly.

I've seen similar things on the baseball field, overzealous coaches so caught up in the competition that they lose sight of the bigger picture. I have confronted youth-league coaches who are still stealing base after base, though they have a twelve-run lead in the third inning. They respond, "Youth-league baseball is different from the pros."

Garbage! Baseball is baseball, and sportsmanship is sportsmanship.

Sure, a youth-league game can quickly turn around and the other team could put up a dozen runs in a blink of an eye. Good! A close game at the youth level is better for all the kids on the field anyhow.

When you have a substantial lead, how about taking out your best pitcher and letting someone pitch who has been wanting to learn how, or letting your full-time right fielder take a shot at shortstop?

How about trying to protect the dignity of the opposing players by not continuing to exploit their weaknesses just so you can brag to the rest of the world that you "destroyed" the other team?

It all comes down to motive. If your motive is to dominate, to embarrass your opponent just to make yourself look better, then you have moved past "sports ignorance." You're just plain ignorant.

We're talking about the developmental years here and what this is all about—teaching, building character, trying to turn kids into adults.

Unfortunately, in many cases the tournament system works against the kind of coaching I'm promoting. In an effort to keep things moving, organizers often seed teams by how many more runs one scores than another. So in essence they're encouraging you to "short game" the other teams (i.e., slaughter them as quickly as you can and save your pitching). That creates terrible gamesmanship. Kids see that if you face somebody weaker, you just keep pounding them.

We fought that. We stopped running, stopped bunting, and put in somebody else to pitch. We weren't trying to let our opponent all the way back into the game, but we at least wanted to make it a challenge, not a humiliation.

As a professional, I agree with the late Vince Lombardi's adage, "Winning isn't everything, it's the only thing." But it's flat wrong to apply that to the amateur level. That's no way to develop kids, but it's a sure bet to eliminate sportsmanship, if that's your aim.

Little League, as an organization, has had this great rule for decades that every kid on the roster gets to play at least two innings. The sad fact is, if it wasn't a rule, you just know there would be plenty of win-at-all-cost coaches—even at that level—who would start their top nine and keep them in the whole game. Those little guys who barely made the team would never play. Why? Because a coach was putting himself and his precious record before his players.

There were times when the shoe was on the other foot, when I would have to go to the opposing coach and say, "Listen, you're running on us, and we have no chance. At what point does this stop being fun? Is there some higher level of satisfaction for you if you beat us by the slaughter rule? Wouldn't it be better if we just kept playing?" But certain coaches apparently loved being able to say, "Hey, we played Matheny's team and we beat them fifteen to nothing."

If you find yourself in that situation, ask yourself if that's really one of the priorities on your list of life's goals. That should give you a good idea what your true motive is for coaching—the kids or your own ego.

We've been given the rare privilege and heavy responsibility of influencing young people on a daily basis, for better or for worse, for the rest of their lives. Which direction will you lead your kids today?

You may still be wondering who I think I am. I get that, and—again—I don't claim to have all the answers. But with Kristin and me having been D-1 scholarship athletes, and with four of our kids either doing the same or on the doorstep, I've seen coaching and parenting done well and I've seen them done poorly. I've already talked a bit about what we've been getting wrong, so now let me share what I think we can do better.

— Part 2 —

A Better Way

4

Our Grand Experiment

Baseball's just a game as simple as a ball and bat, yet as complex as the American spirit it symbolizes. . . . Baseball is cigar smoke, hot roasted peanuts, the *Sporting News,* Ladies' Day, "Down in front!", "Take Me Out to the Ball Game," and "The Star-Spangled Banner." . . . This is a game for America, still a game for America, this baseball!
ADAPTED FROM "THE GAME FOR ALL AMERICA BY ERNIE HARWELL"
(© 1955 BY WILLIAM EARNEST HARWELL)

It's only a coincidence that we launched the Wolverines, who would become the Warriors, right around the time legendary Detroit Tigers play-by-play announcer Ernie Harwell died at ninety-two. You can tell from just the last few paragraphs of the love letter he wrote to baseball fifteen years before I was born that Mr. Harwell was among those who truly revered the game.

What an honor it was to say I knew him. He followed University of Michigan baseball and kept in touch with players who made it to the big leagues. He would go out of his way to come and talk to me whenever I was in Detroit, and I found those conversations surreal after hearing his iconic voice on so many broadcasts.

He always wanted me to call him Ernie, but I just couldn't bring myself to do it. He was so widely respected throughout baseball and, in much the same way as Vin Scully of the Dodgers, revered as a timeless ambassador. Here was a man who believed sports had the potential to rise beyond fun and games and teach lessons that could last a lifetime.

That was our goal with the youth-league Wolverines.

Were we dreaming? Aiming too high? Expecting too much?

We didn't think so. One of our board members, who would eventually have two sons play in our little organization, said, "We don't have this figured out. We don't think we're perfect. We're trying the best we can to change the tenor of youth sports. If you don't shoot really high, you don't get there."

We were asking a lot of the players and their parents. This went way beyond signing some former big leaguer's crazy letter. We requested more than just staying out of the coaching staff's way. We needed the parents' help, and the players had off-the-field requirements, too. Character building involved more than just sitting through studies and discussions, some that I had written and others that I had collected from here and there. We wanted the kids to learn what it meant to help out in the community, too.

So besides getting them used to spending part of every practice without a glove or a bat, learning about honesty or teamwork or loyalty, we looked for service projects. While other teams might be traveling to other states for tournaments, we were looking for places where our boys could help out the less fortunate.

Naturally, anything new and different takes time and comes with its share of bumps in the road. Parents who paid for what looked like it might be fun and exciting had to bear with us as we all had to pitch in. Along the way, we worked together to renovate some retail space for an indoor practice facility; maintain a field that was later donated to us; and find pickup games, as well as other independent teams to play, leagues to join, and tournaments that would accept us.

People who thought we would have fancy uniforms and shoes and gloves and bat bags were sorely disappointed to find that all we invested in were different-colored silk-screened T-shirts (one for home games, another for road games). We said we were emphasizing other things, and we meant it.

When your aim is character and class over glamour and style, it doesn't seem cool. At least at first. And that can drive some people nuts. They get impatient waiting for some evidence of success.

But what does true success look like?

If our program had been about turning out top-drawer, A-list, D-1 scholarship prospects with the big leagues as their ultimate goal, it would have looked entirely different. John Mabry and I might have strutted around in uniforms that looked like we had just stepped out of the majors. Maybe we'd have sunk a bunch of money into facilities and big-name people to train all comers in every aspect of the game. We could have advertised throughout the Midwest and charged thousands of dollars for kids to come and learn how to land on the top scouting lists all over the country.

And to best advertise what we had to offer, we could have sent teams of all-stars to represent us in the best national tournaments we could find.

Such opportunities exist, and they may be just what certain prospects need. But by now you know the odds against a random kid, even the best one in your youth baseball program, actually making it to the big leagues. Finding and grooming that one in a million was not our primary goal. We hoped to maximize the ability of every player we had.

I'm not saying one or more great prospects won't one day come out of what is now known as the Louisville Slugger Warriors, and I'll be as thrilled as anyone. But our purpose from day one was never that, and it still isn't.

Our sole desire was and still is to use the arena of youth sports—in our case, baseball—to teach kids the game, encourage them to love it, and set them on a course toward becoming responsible members of society. Here's how we went about it.

PRACTICES

As I've said, our process can be a slow one. Kids want to play ball. And their parents want to watch them play ball. But we had to prepare them for games, and that meant carefully structured two-hour practice sessions—the first ninety minutes for physical training and the last thirty for mental training and character building.

PHYSICAL

The key to growth at the early stages is repetition, so I tried to get the most work done in the allotted time. I run spring training in the big leagues the same way. We don't waste time. My goal is to have something for every person to do every minute they are on the field. We don't need six hours if we have clear objectives. Stretch, play catch to get your arms loose, do a little conditioning and agility work, and then do the baseball stuff.

Coaches need help, so this is a great time to ask for parent volunteers. I'm amazed how many youth-league teams line up six infielders and hit them one ground ball at a time. That results in low reps, and the kids quickly grow bored. If you don't have parents who can hit ground balls and fly balls, have the boys rotate and hit to each other. In ten minutes, with the boys broken into smaller groups, they will get at least triple the repetitions.

The same with swings. The typical youth-league batting practice is painful. One kid hits while a dozen others are bored out of their minds. Remember, no standing around. While some are working on defense, have the others get in as many swings as possible hitting golf ball–sized plastic balls into a couple of cheap nets.

If you're hitting on the field, have one group work on base running while another is hitting off a tee or hitting soft toss into a net. If you have a fourth group, they can be working on their defense and picking up the batted balls. In an hour and a half, the boys should be exhausted from hustling all over the field and from group to group.

If you're organized and have every minute planned, the kids will get better quicker and you'll sense a buzz—a feeling of urgency—in your workouts.

MENTAL

The last thirty minutes is where our group was unique. This was class time. Many people say baseball is 90 percent mental, but few take the time to train their players for that aspect of the game. We dedicated the first fifteen minutes to the mental side of the game. I used a large white board with a baseball diamond and taught the lesson of the day—maybe cutoffs and relays. I would show where each position player should be on any given play.

If the kids know they have a responsibility aside from the

limited times a ball is actually hit to them, they feel like they are contributing to the success of the team. I believe kids need to see specific plays taught before they are expected to perform them on the field. You can see the excitement level rise when they start to understand the game at this deeper level. We would show them major-league videos and have the boys point out when the pros got it right or wrong.

Other classroom sessions would teach a hitting approach; discuss a pre-at-bat routine, as well as one on deck; or suggest what the kids should do on their own at home between practices. This includes thinking about working the count, moving the runner over, being mindful of the inning, the score, the count, everything.

As the boys get older, they begin to understand the game at a nuanced level, usually increasing their desire to excel at it. Soon they're ready for mental imagery (seeing themselves succeeding), the power of positive thinking, and how to get in the zone for every at bat.

CHARACTER

The final fifteen minutes of our practices were devoted to character studies, which may sound strange but are actually quite simple. Brainstorm the kinds of character traits you want in your own child, or in yourself, and then start making a list. Our topics change every year, as the boys are changing. Topics like honesty, being a good teammate, hard work, and discipline are always applicable. Others, like drugs and alcohol, peer pressure, and sexual purity are conversations for the older boys and can be uncomfortable at first, but these can be real difference makers if the group is engaged in the topic.

I asked a couple of community leaders to prepare fifteen-minute topics of their choice, present them to the boys, and then open it up for discussion. At first all we heard were crickets, but then the boys slowly became involved. It was amazing to be a part of.

How many adults take the time to address these topics with even their own kids? Sadly, too few. We kept parents informed of what we were discussing and invited them to sit in. We asked for their input on these topics and assured them our aim was not to parent their children but to be another adult voice, trying to promote the qualities we all believe are important for our next generation to develop. It was interesting to see the kids slowly realize that here were adults other than their parents who seemed interested in teaching them about life. We publicized, not just to the players but also to parents and anyone interested in what we were doing, these core values that affected everything on and off the field:

1. Service
2. Teamwork
3. Discipline
4. Excellence
5. Responsibility
6. Leadership

We listed these as our nonnegotiables:

- A baseball experience focused on the boys
- Baseball played the right way—with class
- Attitude, concentration, and effort (ACE)—factors the boys can control (with excellence required)
- Biblical truths as our moral compass
- A culture of respect from players, parents, and coaches
- An emphasis on the mental aspect of the game

- The parent's role as a silent source of support
- The players' responsibility to make themselves better

To make these character studies easier to grasp, I often used stories from my childhood and career to bring them to life. In the last part of the book, I'll do the same by sharing some of the lessons we taught, each focusing on a quality the boys could use on and off the field, including leadership, confidence, teamwork, faith, class, character, toughness, and humility.

GIVING BACK

Outside of two hours on the field and in the classroom, we made sure the boys set aside time to practice being good members of the community as well. Our projects included conducting baseball clinics for inner-city kids and helping out with the Challenger League, which was designed for handicapped kids. I was pleased to be able to provide, through my Catch 22 Foundation, a beautiful ball diamond with an artificial track-and-field-type surface accessible to wheelchairs. Our teams annually volunteered as "Angels in the Outfield" to help disabled kids swing the bats and throw. We're very proud of how they have jumped in to help.

We've also had the boys pick up trash on the roadsides, gather recyclables at Cardinals games, and even come up with their own projects to help the less fortunate in their communities—mowing, landscaping, shoveling snow, and handling other such chores for the elderly.

GAMES

Preparation for each game was all about developing a routine, much like what big-league players do. The boys knew what time they needed to show up, and then our goal was efficiency during the pregame routine, just like in practice.

When we played pickup games and instructional games, they were unlike most parents had ever seen—more akin to football scrimmages, because it wasn't uncommon for us to shut things down right in the middle of a play and give either team's coach the chance to explain what happened and what should have happened.

Opposing coaches were dubious at first but then liked the idea of being able to come onto the field and show their pitcher—without having to scream at him or embarrass him from the dugout—that had he backed up his third baseman on the throw from the outfield, the runner would not have scored. Or if the shortstop had rotated to cover third when the third baseman came in to field a bunt, the lead runner might have been cut down at third.

Those coaches also liked the idea of allowing me to point out something their team was doing, and for me to allow them to do the same for our boys. A new voice often makes a big difference. It was a new way to teach baseball, and the kids were learning fast.

During the game, I would also have a different boy sit next to me each inning, and I would challenge him before each pitch: "If you were at shortstop right now, what would you do if the ball was hit on the ground to second?"

I would listen and say, "Okay, but what if he bobbles the ball and the lead runner makes a wide turn at second, where should you be?"

"What if the runner breaks for third and the throw gets past the third baseman. What's your play now? Where are you and what's your job?"

At first the kids were surprised that I wasn't asking them only what they were going to do when the ball was hit to them. I asked that, too, of course; however, the fact is, usually the ball is hit somewhere else, but every player on the field has a specific role every time the ball is put in play. When this finally dawns on them, baseball becomes a whole different game. It's no longer about stretches of boredom while you wait for the ball to come to you. It's all about what you should be thinking about before every pitch, depending on where the ball is hit. We wanted them thinking, *What can I do to help this team win by being prepared for every possibility?*

We had our boys keep a scorebook when they weren't playing, a simple task that gave them an important responsibility and taught them at the same time. Kids get better faster when you teach them in real time during a game, and you won't have bitter kids on the bench. They stay engaged.

To keep things interesting, it also wasn't uncommon for us to change our defensive lineup almost completely. Kids had to learn new positions during a game, and yes, sometimes they were completely lost. You could see parents biting their tongues, and you knew they wanted to say, "But we were ahead when you did that!" Winning wasn't the point—yet. We'd get there, in time. Learning was the point. Learning and fun and teamwork.

Sometimes John Mabry and I would change the lineup by merely moving everyone down one spot every game. In other words, if you led off one game, you batted second the next. That meant if you hit last today, you hit first tomorrow. Eventually our 7-8-9 hitters were hitting 3-4-5. Or if the sixth batter made the last out today, the seventh better would lead off tomorrow. Did that make sense? Not normally, but that didn't matter yet.

We wanted all the kids to experience everything about playing the game. Timid kids who would never volunteer to pitch would be assigned to pitch. They learned things about themselves, about pitching, and about teamwork.

We didn't keep any stats. I kept urging the parents, "You're going to have a tendency to try and keep stats, so you can say at the end of the year that Johnny hit .650 or whatever. I want to discourage that, because it works against everything we're trying to accomplish."

It's important that we teach players that they're never really as good or as bad as their statistics might indicate. Kevin Seitzer, a Milwaukee Brewers teammate my rookie year and my first big-league mentor, advised me to never read the papers. He said, "You're never as bad as they say you are when things are going bad, and you're never as good as they say you are when things are going well."

That's great wisdom I've tried to pass on to the Cardinals every year. A box score might show one player going 0-4 and another going 4-4 with four RBIs. A bad night for one and a great night for the other, right? Maybe, statistically. But one may have hit the ball hard all four times and been robbed every time, while the other saw bloopers and ground balls find holes.

My oldest son, Tate, went through that his first year at Missouri State. He was Freshman of the Year for the Missouri Valley Conference and Team MVP, leading in nearly every offensive category. But I saw some of his games, and frankly, he was swinging at everything and getting some ugly two-strike hits. He had a lot of strikeouts, but he hit .336, and it seemed every time he put the ball in play it was a hit.

I'm aware of the pressure of being the son of a former big leaguer and a manager, and I sure didn't want to bust his confidence. But when a kid's results are so good, it's hard to convince him he's doing anything wrong. As a speedy center fielder, I knew that for Tate to keep advancing he would be expected to produce offensively and be an on-base guy.

When he started summer ball, I urged him, "Make sure you're working on putting the ball in play and fighting those two strikes. To keep getting on base consistently, you're going to have to really work your strike zone and coax some walks."

So over the summer he did that, and though he was getting the barrel of the bat on everything, he often hit it right at somebody, so his average was a little under .300. He'd call me and ask, "What am I doing?"

I told him, "You're having a better season than last year, regardless of your average. Stick with the process. This game may be about results to everyone on the outside, but as soon as you start trying to change, you'll be going in a bad direction. You're not striking out. You're doing exactly what you're supposed to be doing. Those hits are going to start to fall."

His sophomore season at Missouri State, he was among the top twenty-five hardest to strike out in Division 1, cut his 54-game strikeout total from 47 to just 19, hit .330, was Team MVP again, and made first team All Conference. That summer he was named to the 24-man USA Baseball's Collegiate National Team.

How this plays out with young boys is in how they view their performance as opposed to how their parents and others see it. Sometimes, when they don't accomplish what some of the more advanced kids do, they focus on the negative. Then it becomes our job to make sure the boys and their families understand the improvement we've seen and the contribution they've made to the team. Stats are very important at the professional level, but even all our in-depth analytics don't tell the whole story. A player may be doing much more for his team than the stats reveal.

Similarly, in those early days we often didn't keep score. There were even times when I'd keep our team out on defense and let the other team hit through their order twice. Sure, they were going to score runs, but we were working on defensive positioning, backups, and other things. Not only did I know we were going to lose those games, I made sure of it.

While we got our teeth kicked in early, as we learned, we started to see a little success with this plan. We slowly built the kids up and then went back and played some of those teams we played in the beginning. It worked out well, because we found we were very competitive by the end of the season.

Once we started playing in earnest, our kids made us proud by showing us they had learned not only to play well and to play smart but also to play with class. Win or lose, they treated one another well, respected their opponents and the umpires, and impressed tournament and league officials wherever we went. I recently heard that one of the boys from our program had been recruited to play ice hockey for the University of Wisconsin. His father tells me that one of the Wisconsin coaches told him they had been impressed with the fact that not only was this young man a great player, but he also shook the hands of the referees after every game and was the only player to do so. The coach said he asked the boy why he did that and was told, "I was taught to respect the umpires on my youth-league baseball team and to shake their hands after every game."

You can imagine how gratifying it was to hear that story.

Most of the boys who pass through our program will not play professional or even college ball, but they'll know what it means to be a disciplined, selfless, service-oriented contributor to society. I hope they'll be people of character, like the men I met a couple of years ago when I got to visit the Naval Special Warfare Unit in Coronado, California.

I was there with players and coaches from the Cardinals and found it one of the most eye-opening experiences I'd ever had. When we arrived, a group of servicemen in their second week of determining whether they had the right stuff to become elite Navy SEALs was pulling themselves off the beach, carrying their rafts.

Thirty-five had already drubbed themselves out of the competition, deciding it wasn't for them. The rest were into day two of the second week of a four-week weeding-out process that challenged their minds as much as their bodies. Those who survived the four weeks would have to endure one more week-long test, during which they would be allowed only four hours of sleep (two on Wednesday and two on Thursday) while being put through more mental and physical testing.

All just to become one of the select few honored with the SEAL name.

We spent the day talking with established veteran SEALs, and it was obvious there was something different about them. I asked one, who had served with multiple different SEAL teams as both a leader and an instructor, what were the characteristics he commonly saw in those who made it through the process and were selected. He listed the following five:

1. Physical toughness ("The easiest quality to find," he said.)
2. Mental toughness
3. Moral toughness (He described this as "Doing the right thing all the time, even when nobody's looking.")

4. Team orientation ("A belief that the needs of the team are greater than your own.")

5. Humility

Now, there's a list that can be applied to any area of life. That'll work at home, in the office, on the team, anywhere. And it sure reinforces the need for coaches to help raise high-character kids. They may not be destined for the big leagues, but they just may make a difference in the boardroom and, who knows, maybe even become modern-day heroes who fight for our freedom.

ON WINNING

Now, before you lump me with those who think every kids' game ought to end in a tie and everybody ought to get a trophy, let me set the record straight. That's not where I'm coming from at all.

I've spent a lot of time criticizing coaches and parents who focus too much on winning, especially at the youngest ages, and I stand by that. But I do believe that in sports, as in everything else, there needs to be balance.

The idea that everyone is a winner and should have fun is fine for a child's first or second year of organized sports—what's the sense in discouraging and frustrating and humiliating a little kid who's just trying to figure out the game?

But by a certain age there is way too much to learn from loss and failure to let kids continue thinking that everyone should get a trophy, even when they finish in last place. A participation ribbon, sure. A certificate that says they spent their summer playing, fine. But a trophy? Come on, now.

If you want to teach a kid a life skill, teach him reality. Give him a picture of what the world will throw his way. Even the rich and famous have their share of heartache and loss. People go broke. People get sick. Loved ones die. There are setbacks, cutbacks, rollbacks, buyouts, layoffs, bankruptcies. Is it fair to reward a kid for everything he does until he's eighteen, filling his room with trophies regardless how he performs, and then find him shocked the first time he fails a course or loses a girlfriend or gets fired from a job?

No, sorry, that guy got the big trophy and you got the skinny little white ribbon because his team kicked your tail. Deal with it.

The point here is not that we should make sure everybody feels warm and fuzzy and no one's feelings get hurt. The bigger picture is teaching a person to put on his big-boy pants and learn to handle failure.

Due to its very nature, baseball is a great instructor on this topic. One of the oldest adages in the book is about how even the greatest players in the history of the game have failed 70 percent of the time at the plate.

To make that clear, consider this: of the tens of thousands of players who have played major-league baseball in its history, the all-time highest career batting average was achieved by Ty Cobb at .366.

Anyone who knows the game understands how incredible that is, to maintain such a lofty average over a lifetime of playing at the highest level. But think of it. For every thousand official at bats, the best-hitting player in history was put out 634 times! He failed 63.4 percent of the time!

What separates the great players from the others is not just that they fail less frequently but how they handle it when they do. They see their shortfalls, figure out ways to fix them, and jump right back into the fight. In baseball terms, they make adjustments more quickly than other players. Developing such skill sets did not come without facing many setbacks.

In my personal life as well as my professional life, I have—without doubt—learned more from failure than from success. I'm guessing the same is true for you. If I'm right, why are we parents and coaches so afraid to let our kids face a little adversity?

We need to step aside and let them fail, and then be quick to help redirect their efforts. Then, *after* they have invested sweat and tears and the discipline of hard work into really achieving something, the trophy they actually *earn* will mean that much more to them.

More important, the lessons learned by striving to improve and achieve will be skills they can use the rest of their lives.

WHEN I THINK of people who have overcome adversity and have achieved in spite of everything, it's hard to top the example of Jackie Robinson, who broke the color barrier in major-league baseball. When Kristin and I saw the movie *42,* it instantly became my favorite baseball picture ever. I knew the story, but the movie did a great job of bringing it to life.

But the best part was not the movie itself. It happened that the only other person in the theater that night was an elderly black man, and throughout the movie he cheered and sometimes wept. At the end he strode out of that theater looking as if he had personally identified with the struggles Jackie Robinson had gone through. It was obvious he had been watching a movie about his hero.

As we left, he went out of his way to approach me. "What'd you think of the movie?" he said.

"One of the best I've ever seen, sir," I said.

He just kept walking, a huge smile on his face. "I agree, son."

Amazing what the game of baseball has done and can continue to do in people's lives. Jackie Robinson was more than a pioneer and a courageous athlete. He embodied hope for countless people. I'm sure Jackie had some idea what an important role he was playing nearly seventy years ago, but I wonder if he ever imagined the monumental difference he has made in our world.

You and I are just parents and coaches not likely to ever have anywhere near the influence Number 42 did. But let's not sell ourselves short with regard to the impact we can have on the people who look up to us every day—our own kids and the kids we teach and coach. They're looking for someone to stand up for what is right and to make a difference in their lives. That's what heroes can do, and it starts with having the courage to do things differently.

5

Parents Just Trying to Get It Right

People who know me—I mean really know me—will find it strange that I have written a book. I've never cared about being in the spotlight, being known, being somebody. Don't get me wrong, I want to make a difference and I strive to do things with excellence, but it really never has been to make a name for myself. The part of managing I like best is helping others succeed and seeing a team come together to accomplish something.

That doesn't seem to add up, I know, because being a major-league manager alone puts me in a fraternity of only thirty men. Becoming manager of the St. Louis Cardinals (second only to the Yankees in World Series championships won) made me a *very* public person almost overnight. It comes with the territory, and I accept as part of my job that I must face the press both before and after every game and answer for every move I make—or don't make, for that matter.

Some people love and thrive in the public nature of such a role. More power to them. I'd be just as thrilled to have my job if nobody knew my name. But just as I bite the bullet and cheerfully (usually) face the reporters every day, I leave my comfort zone here, too, and beg your pardon as I say more about myself than I would under any other circumstance. I will say that where I grew up, how I grew up, the family I grew up in, the parents who raised me—all contribute to the way I see things. They're why I'm considered old school, though I was born in 1970, and they also shape my beliefs about what good sports parents get right.

GO OUTSIDE AND PLAY!

The Mathenys wound up in that suburb on the east side of Columbus because my dad had moved north, chasing his own baseball dream from a West Virginia farm to the big city. When that didn't pan out, he became a heavy-equipment operator, and he and Mom raised us four boys in a 1,200-square-foot house they still live in.

If your dad "worked construction" or was "blue collar" or "drove a truck"—that quaint expression people use for a workin' man—you probably also know what it means to "pull six twelves." That's what my dad did most of the summers I was growing up, and it meant what it sounds like: he worked six twelve-hour days every week, leaving home long before dawn and getting back at dinnertime.

That's why it meant something when I said he didn't just eat and collapse in an easy chair for the rest of the evening. And that wasn't all. In a house that size, there was no hiding anything, which was what was so impressive about my parents. Not one time did I ever hear them raise their voices to each other. I know there had to be issues. Money was always tight, especially with four hungry boys, so I know things weren't always as smooth as they seemed.

Make no mistake about it, they were very consistent people—consistent in how they treated each other and in how they treated us. Humble, honest, and dependable is the way I would describe them. Dad worked for the same company for thirty-eight years, and Mom still works for the church ministry she has served since I was a kid. And as hard as Dad worked, it's not like he really took Sundays off. He picked up kids in the inner city for church and taught Sunday school. I know that was way out of his comfort zone, quiet as he was. My brothers and I were basically raised in church. We were there Sunday morning, Sunday night, and Wednesday night, which gave us a great foundation, and we knew what was expected of us.

Dad was the disciplinarian, no question. Mom tried to keep most of our knuckleheaded antics from him, particularly when he was frazzled, but she wasn't above dropping a wait-till-your-dad-gets-home on us, and none of us wanted that. I never wanted to disappoint my dad, and I especially looked forward to the time we spent together, practicing baseball, when he got home. Despite his tough days, he still made it a priority to help me improve.

Parents on our first Wolverines team often asked me what they should do to help their child improve. I think they were eager for me to tell them where to take their son for pitching lessons or hitting lessons or strength training. My response usually surprised them, and I know it challenged them. I suggested they play catch with their child, hit him grounders and pop flies—just as my dad did with me.

To develop skills, the younger player needs repetition. For life in general, he needs time with his parents. It's a win-win.

The temptation these days is to consider it a huge victory to get kids out of the house, off their computers, away from their smartphones, out from in front of any screen long enough to do what we did when we were kids—just play.

But don't just send them outside. When was the last time you went outside to play *with* your kids? I know we're all busy, and our schedules are so full that playing outside with them seems impossible. But if you've read this far, that tells me you're willing to accept the challenge to make some changes.

You don't need an expert to tell you that kids stay inside way too much. I'm sure you're aware of the childhood obesity epidemic related to kids not getting enough exercise. But didn't at least one or two of your greatest childhood memories include your mom or dad, or both, going outside with you and doing what, _____ (you fill in the blank)?

I can tell you that my favorite memories involve my family making up games in the backyard, or hunting and fishing. Besides the Wiffle ball games I've already told you about, there were all kinds of other games that Mom or Dad were part of, and I believe those times helped me develop skills that allowed me to play sports at higher levels later. But even if they hadn't, just as important, I got to spend time with the people I loved. Plus, it was just plain fun. The hours would fly by, and the only thing I worried about was how much longer we could play before it got dark.

Why don't we do that anymore?

Frankly, it's hard to blame the kids. If they're in charge of what goes on in your family, you've got bigger problems than how you act at their ball games.

I know it's easy to just let them fall into an Xbox coma so we can get all our "important" things done. But fast-forward a few years and imagine they're off to college or the military or have their own family, and ask yourself if whatever kept you from that outside time seems so important now.

It's a trap we all fall into, but ask your kids if they'd like to go out and shoot some hoops or throw a ball around. I think you know how they'll respond. And even when you really can't go outside with them, you're still doing your kids a huge favor by making them go.

Kristin and I had our five fairly close together, meaning we had the fun—and the challenge—of having five teenagers all at the same time, too. But now that they're starting to leave the nest one by one, it's hitting us how fleeting are those opportunities to spend time with the greatest gift we were ever given.

You may be saying that your kids are already too old and you missed your chance. Well, I've heard it said that the best time to plant a tree is twenty years ago—and the second-best time is right now. If you haven't done a good job of going outside and playing with your kids, start a new tradition today. Whether your children are teenagers or toddlers . . .

Go outside and play!

YOUTH ISN'T ALWAYS WASTED . . .

With a late-September birthday, I was one of those kids whose parents were given the option to start me in kindergarten at age four, which can have its advantages and disadvantages. In my case, I'm glad my parents chose to have me start early; it worked out for the best in the long run. Maybe they weren't consciously thinking about what I would face down the road, but I doubt they worried about any size or age disadvantage, especially given my place in a family of boys. Sure, there were the awkward stages when kids lost their baby teeth before I did, started growing taller before I did, and began going through puberty before I did. But being a little younger and smaller forced me to compete harder in sports and made me a better athlete. In the end I was grateful for what looked like a drawback at the time. Probably without intending to, my parents had given me a mental edge, forcing me to become more determined if I wanted to compete.

My brothers and I played every sport possible, and my next-older brother was a good athlete, so that was a challenge for me, too. There wasn't a lot to do in a small house like ours, so when we weren't at church, we were on the playground at the elementary school a couple of hundred yards away.

Baseball started for me in 1977 with tee ball when I was six years old. The coach would put me on the pitcher's mound (naturally, with kids hitting off a tee, there was no pitching), and I was that kid the other kids' parents hated because I would run all over the field to make plays. The coach should have stopped me and let the other kids learn, but I'm sure he thought I represented our best chance to win. Here it was, tee ball, and he was making a big deal of the fact that we went unbeaten that whole season.

Of course, I didn't know any better and thought it was pretty cool. I was the fastest guy out there. I could catch the ball and I could throw it, so the problem was finding somebody who could catch it at first base. All I remember is people being upset because I was running in front of their kid to make plays. Maybe that's one reason I'm so insistent about this now. You can't expect six- and seven-year-olds to see what's wrong with that picture.

At the end of the season we got trophies and had a parade in which our team, the Tigers, got to ride on a truck that had been dolled up like a striped Bengal, and I thought that this baseball stuff was pretty great.

After another year of tee ball, I got to face live pitching. But best of all, my dad was the coach. Those were two great years when I was eight and nine. There's a picture at my grandmother's house of me in my first game as a catcher wearing a big old hat like a train conductor, chest protector dragging on the ground between my knees, shin guards hanging off to the side, one buckle intact on each.

This experience also links with another common factor among professional athletes: many of us were forced to play against older, better competition. Too many naturally talented kids enjoy dominating a team or even a league for years, and then they're sorely disappointed when they finally get to the next level and face equal competition. They've never been stretched.

That's why I'm grateful I was a late bloomer and one of the smallest in my class. It made me work harder just to survive. I often wonder what would have happened to all of those over-sized twelve-year-olds out there, whose early success stalled out later, if a parent or coach had just found the proper competition for them.

This is a tough topic, because we want our kids to have fun and play with their friends, but we also want to see them succeed. The problem starts when an early-developed child is left at a lower level to continue dominating, or a coach rationalizes keeping him there so he can keep putting trophies on the shelf.

It's time for someone to make a tough decision. It's hard for a coach to show enough character to tell a star's parents their child should play at a higher level, but it's the right thing to do.

If athletes are not pushed, they will not grow. I see it even at the professional level, when guys who have always been able to out-talent the competition are suddenly put into an environment with equally talented players who have overcome obstacles or failure. Guess who comes out on top?

Legendary college basketball coach Bobby Knight once told me he did not watch his potential recruits play just basketball but also other sports. He wanted to see them play a sport in which they would not be the best and needed to fight and work to improve. On a high school basketball court he knew they would dominate, but how would a 6'7" power forward compete on a baseball field? Interesting perspective. Are you properly pushing your kids?

THE VALUE IN VARIETY

When baseball season was over, we'd do the Wiffle ball thing in the backyard or we'd throw a football around or go to the school and learn some life lessons on the basketball court. I was never any good, but all you needed was a ball. I had started young falling in love with competing, and it was good that my parents had not limited me to baseball. I later found that I had that in common with other big leaguers. A lot of us also had siblings who pushed us hard, and we weren't sport-specific until later.

People made a big deal of football in central Ohio, and that area tended to produce some good players. Our city seemed to shut down for high school football, and as I got older and bigger, I found I could throw the ball pretty well. As a junior I became the starting quarterback at Reynoldsburg High, and I began getting some looks from a few different colleges. Down deep I knew I was a little better at baseball, yet I couldn't help but be drawn to the excitement that went along with football.

However, while I loved the benefits, the competition, practices, and the camaraderie—I worked my way into becoming an okay football player—I didn't really love the game the way I did baseball. Still, I think there's a lesson here about not specializing too soon. I could have burned out on baseball had I become a single-sport athlete before I graduated from high school. I actually had an elite soccer club coach approach me about one of my own sons when he was nine years old and try to convince me the best thing for him would be to drop every other sport and commit to soccer year-round. Of course, I was honored that he thought so highly of my son, but then he rattled off his credentials while "guaranteeing" my son would be a Division 1 player "if he committed to it."

Hockey experts tried to convince me the same boy needed to focus on hockey in order to reach the next level.

I never gave that any serious thought, because this kid loved moving from one sport to the next, depending on the weather and the season. One year he tired of baseball and wanted to focus on hockey. Eventually he was drafted by a professional baseball team and signed a scholarship to play collegiately. It was his decision and his timing, not mine, when he figured out what he loved to do.

I'm grateful my parents let me transition from football to basketball to baseball each year. What a mistake it would have been to push my kids in any one direction at an early age.

The trainer for the Cardinals, Greg Hauck, agrees and offered some thoughts on the best ways for kids to develop athleticism while avoiding injury. He says the most important thing for them to do is to just play. "Kids forget to play. That's going to help develop their athleticism, versus all the specific baseball camps (pitching camp, hitting camp, etc.).

"If you let them play, they learn to move in more efficient

ways, versus doing one thing over and over again. Repetitive action predisposes them to injury.

"Kids are still in the developmental stage. They may be able to handle some strength training, but if they're under fourteen, I recommend body-weight strength training like push-ups, pull-ups, and sit-ups. That's about all they need, because they're going to get stronger just based on their natural development. Anything more could affect their structure at this age. Real weight training can wait till after puberty."

THE POWER OF TRYING SOMETHING NEW

It was obvious baseball was special to our extended family, too, when they would come all the way from West Virginia to watch us play. It was a great family, and even at a young age, I could see there was a level of respect that went along with being able to do something well.

As a baseball man himself, Dad could see even back then that I had some skills. He sat me down one day before my last summer playing for him, when I was ten, and said, "You like this baseball stuff, don't you?"

I nodded.

"You know, if you want to go as far as you can, the best way to do it is as a catcher."

I liked that idea. "Yeah, I'll do that."

It's a funny thing about catching. Some great players, and I mean even big leaguers, can't do it. I don't mean just that they're not good at it. I mean they can't do it at all. They blink or they flinch when the batter swings, so while they could probably fill in for an inning or two at virtually any other position on the field if they had to, they couldn't fill in at catcher for even one out.

And they know it, too. With the Cardinals, I always have to figure out who's going to be our emergency guy if our starter and backups somehow go down. I have to find someone who's either done a little bit of catching at some level or is at least willing, just in case. Every manager has to do that. In fact, it's one of the interview questions we use to figure out who's going to be on our team. I say, "Hey, if we get in a bind, will you get behind the plate?"

It's amazing how many professionals will say, "Sorry, there's no way I could do that."

I did push the kids on our youth team to try new positions at least once. After trying it, even catching, they would often admit that it wasn't so bad. I was careful, though, not to put them in positions where they were sure to get hurt. If they were really young and couldn't catch the ball, I wouldn't put them behind the plate or at first base. Neither would I put a kid behind the plate who was afraid to catch. And I wouldn't put a boy with slow reactions in the infield when the opposing team was hitting lasers. I had to pick and choose where I exposed kids to new positions.

I do believe kids should start specializing in certain positions at some point, but not until they are well into their teenage years. We're seeing kids just getting started in the game who are told they are "pitcher only." Are you kidding me? These kids can't even know which position they might be most interested in, and someone has already decided for them. Please, let them play all the positions at the beginning stages of their games, and I'm talking about more than tee ball.

Best is to have the kids list the positions they'd love to play and then ask which ones they'd like to learn more about. I suggest that coaches tell each of the kids that the team needs them to pitch so that none of the other kids will end up hurting their arms from overwork.

The less-talented kids often shy away from pitching, because it's such a visible and high-pressure position. But once they get out there and throw a few strikes and get some outs, they are proud of themselves and feel like a big part of the team. They'll soon see that they can do it and will start working harder on their throwing skills and become better overall players in the long run.

So I CAUGHT that whole season for my dad's team, and near the end of the summer of 1981 was named to the all-star team. There I was noticed by a man named Ron Golden, a former catcher in the San Francisco minor-league system, who was looking for players he could develop into a traveling team and whom he would eventually use to help him teach baseball camps. He still does this all over central Ohio, but this was his first group.

When Coach Golden asked my dad if I could join his program and play for his team, I found out quickly how important my catching was to Dad. I've told you how mild-mannered and soft-spoken he was. Well, he was also tough and strong and would never talk to a coach unless he was asked. In this case, he went out of his way to talk to Mr. Golden.

After having seen another coach overuse my brother Rusty as a pitcher and hurt him, Dad said, "I know Michael has a good arm, but if he's going to play for you, I'd rather he not pitch very often."

I knew that was hard for him to even say, because he believed—as I do now—that the coach should have the freedom to play kids wherever he feels they best contribute to the team. He knew Mr. Golden had seen me catching on the all-star team, and he just wanted to make sure I didn't end up on the mound all the time and blow up my arm. I did in fact pitch a few innings here and there and played other positions from time to time, and my dad was fine with that. I appreciate that he had the courage to ask and the wisdom to know when to step away.

I wasn't sure at first how much I would get to catch for Coach Golden, because his own son, Eric, a year younger than I, was also a catcher. At our first practice/tryout, he stood us next to each other, had us put on catcher's gear, grabbed a bucket of balls and a fungo bat, and started whacking balls at us from close range to block.

It wasn't long before I was crying under the mask, thinking, *I gotta do this!* and realizing his son didn't like it much either. The drill didn't last long, and I still don't know if it was a test or what. For all I know, Coach Golden had to prove to himself that I was the better catcher. He wound up putting Eric at shortstop, and years later he went on to play at the University of Central Florida as a second baseman for his whole college career.

By 1983, the summer I was twelve, I was playing my second season for Coach Golden, definitely a cut above everybody else as far as coaching goes. He gathered the team after a game and began reviewing how we had done—as he always did. He evaluated the season so far and talked about the state of the team, and I don't know what drove him to say it, but he just blurted, ". . . and we have the best catcher in the entire state of Ohio."

I sat there stunned. *Does he really think that?*

I was playing with this whole talented group of kids, and I wondered why he would say that. He was a former professional catcher himself, a man who knew the talent around the state, a person who never said things just to hear himself talk.

That one sentence told me, even at that young age, that I had a chance, and I was determined to make the most of it.

Thinking back to that day now I realize that, even though my parents worked hard to keep me grounded, a coach is in such a powerful position to shape an impressionable young mind—for harm or for good—with just one comment. All the more reason you need to be able to recognize the good ones when you see them.

6

What a Great Coach Looks Like

I can't think of a coach or manager of any significant program or organization who won't tell you he owes something to the godfather of old-school coaching, John Wooden. In fact, some refer to this man as the fountainhead of successful modern leadership, and they don't even limit it to sports.

fountainhead *1. a spring from which a stream flows; the head or source of a stream; 2. a chief source of anything*

I could write another whole book alone about the coaches who've taught me so much. In fact, I'll mention them throughout, because I don't want this to be only about me.

But John Wooden also happens to be the coach to whom I owe the most, the one whose approach and philosophy I work hardest to imitate, though we never met. And I won't meet him this side of heaven, because he died four months short of his one hundredth birthday, in 2010.

Not one of my own former coaches will resent me for putting

him at the top of my list, because he's probably at the top of theirs, too. You can't do better than to pattern your coaching—and your life—after John Wooden.

You won't even find it strange that a baseball manager idolizes a basketball coach. But let me tell you what was unique about Coach Wooden and why so many strive to be like him. In a nutshell, he became one of the winningest coaches in history by emphasizing character over winning.

Think of it. The man *never* talked of winning! He didn't even think winning was the point. To him winning was just the evidence, the result of doing things the right way.

In his own words: "I felt that if the players were prepared, we would do just fine. If we won, great—frosting on the cake. But at no time did I consider winning to be the cake. Winning has always been the frosting that made the cake a little tastier."

If we won, great?! This from the coach whose teams won more than 80 percent of their games over his last twenty-seven years?

So if he didn't talk about winning, what did he talk about?

He talked about character.

He talked about teamwork.

He talked about humility and sacrifice and selflessness and process.

He even talked about success.

But do you know what success meant to John Wooden? You'll find as I tell his story that he spent years coming to this conclusion, but in the end he said, "Success is peace of mind, which is a direct result of self-satisfaction in knowing you made the effort to become the best of which you are capable."

So simple, yet so profound.

Now, just in case you don't know who John Wooden was: As

head basketball coach of UCLA—the "Wizard of Westwood"—from 1948 to 1975, he led the Bruins to ten NCAA national championships in his last twelve years, seven of those in a row—something never done before or since. During that time, the Bruins once won a record eighty-eight straight games, and Wooden was named national coach of the year six times.

So how did a coach who seemingly emphasized everything but winning win so much?

At age twenty-four, he accepted a position coaching and teaching English at South Bend Central High School—where he grew frustrated with the grading system and searched for a way to assure his students and their parents they could be successful without earning all A's.

"I wanted to give them something to aspire to beyond higher marks in English classes or more statistics in sports," he said.

Wooden believed true success ought to be tied not to achievement, wealth, or fame but to how close a person came to their potential. He wanted his students to see success not in terms of results but in terms of effort.

John Wooden's first definition of success I quoted above satisfied him for a while, but he wanted something more concrete. He spent the next fourteen years coming up with fifteen different behaviors necessary to achieve real success and arranged them in a diagram now known as John Wooden's Pyramid of Success. From top to bottom, the behaviors include competitive greatness, poise, confidence, condition, skill, team spirit, self-control, alertness, initiative, intentness, industriousness, friendship, loyalty, cooperation, and enthusiasm.

Wooden's principles were put to the test after he took the UCLA job for the 1948–1949 season. Before signing a three-year contract there, he had been in line for head coach at Minnesota, the job he really wanted because he and his wife preferred to stay in the Midwest. Somehow bad weather delayed the Golden Gophers in getting back to Wooden, so he assumed they had lost interest.

Just after he took the job at UCLA, the people at Minnesota reached him and made him an attractive offer. Naturally, he felt duty-bound to UCLA because he had given his word.

When head coach Mel Taube left Purdue in 1950 and Wooden was asked to come back, he would have loved to have taken that job. But he could not and would not, because leaving UCLA before his three-year contract expired would have been breaking his word.

When was the last time you heard of a little thing like that standing in a coach's way?

As they say, John Wooden did more than just talk the talk.

By then he had already made a name for himself as an unconventional coach. He wasn't a screamer, and he was methodical to the point where his new players were at first amused. He started by showing them how to dress for practice and for a game, including how to put on their socks and shoes. It seemed ridiculous until he explained how important it was for them to avoid blisters and cutting off the circulation in their feet. He was known to say, "There are little details in everything you do, and if you get away from any one of those little details, you're not teaching the thing as a whole. For it is little things which, together, make the whole."

With his strangely quiet manner, hardly ever rising from the bench, a game program rolled in his fist and arms folded, the soft-spoken Wooden was one who believed that coaching was done between games, during practice. The 1963–1964 season became the first of his four 30-0s and the first of those ten national championships over the next twelve years.

In John Wooden's second-to-last season, UCLA finished third in the finals in 1974, losing in double overtime in the semis to eventual champion North Carolina State.

They won it all again in 1975, the year Wooden retired, giving him his eighth national championship in nine years and tenth in the last twelve. The coach wrote in his biography that on his way off the court, a UCLA fan approached him and said, "This makes up for letting us down last year."

His teams had won 620 of 767 games in twenty-seven seasons, an .808 winning percentage.

Though he won too many honors and awards to mention—including NCAA College Basketball Coach of the Year in 1964, 1967, 1969, 1970, 1971, 1972, and 1973, and 1972's *Sports Illustrated* magazine's Sportsman of the Year—he never made more than $35,000 a year in salary and reportedly never asked for a raise. In 2009, John Wooden was named Greatest Coach of All Time by the *Sporting News*.

CLEARLY, COACH WOODEN'S record is unparalleled. But by now you know I don't admire him for that. What makes me wish I had met him—and, yes, makes me want to be like him—is the way he defined success. To him it was all about character, the intangibles, doing the right things because they are the right things.

Do that, and winning takes care of itself.

This man has had more influence on my coaching than anyone else, because he proved his theories by modeling them in his own life. All those building blocks on his Pyramid of Success are his own character traits. The people who knew him best say he was a loyal friend, cooperative, enthusiastic, and industrious. He showed self-control, poise, and confidence, but always with humility.

He was a devout Christian and often said his beliefs were more important to him than basketball: "Basketball is not the ultimate. It is of small importance in comparison to the total life we live. There is only one kind of life that truly wins, and that is the one that places faith in the hands of the Savior."

He was a daily Bible reader and a member of the First Christian Church. He once said, "If I were ever prosecuted for my religion, I truly hope there would be enough evidence to convict me."

John Wooden wrote many books about leadership, success, basketball, and life, and many others have been written about him. I have only hinted here at the depth of the man, so I would urge you to Google his name and see what's available.

He coached many famous players who went on to the NBA, the two most famous being Lew Alcindor (Kareem Abdul-Jabbar) and Bill Walton. His players loved him and especially appreciated his quips and inspirational quotes, several of which I'll list here. Coach Wooden never claimed they were all original with him, but it seemed he had one for every occasion. Bill Walton says he used to write these on his sons' lunch bags when he sent them off to school.

JOHN WOODEN'S MAXIMS

ON TIME

- Be quick, but don't hurry.
- If you don't have time to do it right, when will you find the time to do it over?
- Good things take time, as they should. We shouldn't expect good things to happen overnight. Getting something too easily or too soon can cheapen the outcome.
- Don't let yesterday take up too much of today.
- Time lost is lost forever. People tell themselves they will work twice as hard tomorrow to make up for what they did not do today. People should always do their best. If they work twice as hard tomorrow, then they should have also worked twice as hard today. That would have been their best.

ON PUTTING OTHERS FIRST

- Seek opportunities to show you care. The smallest gestures often make the biggest difference.
- Be more concerned with what you can do for others than what others can do for you. You'll be surprised at the results.
- You cannot live a perfect day without doing something for another without thought of something in return.
- Happiness begins where selfishness ends.
- Sincerity may not help us make friends, but it will help us keep them.
- We can give without loving, but we can't love without giving. In fact, love is nothing unless we give it to someone.

ON PERSONAL GROWTH

- Many athletes have tremendous God-given gifts, but they don't focus on the development of those gifts. Who are they? You've never heard of them, and you never will. It's true in sports, and it's true in life.

- If you keep too busy learning the tricks of the trade, you may never learn the trade.

- The more concerned we become over the things we can't control, the less we will do with the things we can control.

- Perfection is what you are striving for, but perfection is an impossibility. However, *striving* for perfection is not an impossibility.

- The best competition I have is against myself to become better.

- We get stronger when we test ourselves. Adversity can make us better. We must be challenged to improve, and adversity is the challenger.

ON CHARACTER

- Ability may get you to the top, but character keeps you there. Your character is what you really are; your reputation is merely what others think you are.

- It is what you learn after you know it all that counts.

- Players with fight never lose a game; they just run out of time.

- Be most interested in finding the best way, not in having your own way.

- Never make excuses. Your friends don't need them, and your foes won't believe them.

- You are no better than anyone else, and no one is better than you.

ON THE SPIRITUAL LIFE

- I've never stopped trying to do what's right. I'm not doing it to earn favor with God. I'm doing it because it's the right thing to do.
- If we magnified blessings as much as we magnify disappointments, we would all be much happier.
- Being true to ourselves doesn't make us people of integrity. Charles Manson was true to himself, and as a result, he rightly is spending the rest of his life in prison. Ultimately, being true to our Creator gives us the purest form of integrity.
- I wanted my players to always be searching, especially for truth. I wanted them to know what they believed and be able to defend it. Truth will always stand the test of scrutiny.
- If I did only what I wanted to do, I would not be obedient to the Creator. Sometimes He wants us to do certain things that we may not feel like doing. When it comes to what God asks of us, we need more than good intentions—we need to follow through fully.
- You can do more good by being good than any other way.

ON FAILURE

- Success is never final. Failure is never fatal. It's courage that counts.
- The man who is afraid to risk failure seldom has to face success.
- Don't permit fear of failure to prevent effort. We are all imperfect and will fail on occasion, but fear of failure is the greatest failure of all.
- Second-guessing yourself is wasted effort. Does worrying over it change it? Nope, it just wastes your time. And if

you complain about it to others, you're wasting their time. Nothing is gained by wasting all that time.

- I expected my players to make mistakes, as long as they were mistakes of commission. A mistake of commission happens when you are doing what should be done but don't get the results you want.

- Close games are usually lost, rather than won. What I mean by that is that games are mostly won because the opponent makes mistakes during crucial moments.

ON TEAMWORK

- We don't have to be superstars or win championships. All we have to do is learn to rise to every occasion, give our best effort, and make those around us better as we do it.

- We can become great in the eyes of others, but we'll never become successful if we compromise our character and show disloyalty toward friends or teammates. The reverse is also true: no individual or team will become great without loyalty.

- Understanding that the good of the group comes first is fundamental to being a highly productive member of a team.

- Much can be accomplished by teamwork when no one is concerned about who gets credit.

- Kindness makes for much better teamwork.

ON COACHING

- The coach is first of all a teacher.

- It's impossible to claim you have taught if there are students who have not learned. With that commitment, from my first year as an English teacher until my last as UCLA basketball teacher/coach, I was determined to make the effort to become the best teacher I could possibly be, not for my sake, but for all those who were placed under my supervision.

- I never yelled at my players much. Artificial stimulation doesn't last long. It's like love and passion. Passion won't last as long as love. It's the same with yelling.

- Approval is a greater motivator than disapproval, but we have to disapprove on occasion when we correct. I make corrections only after I have proved to the individual that I highly value him. If they know we care for them, our correction won't be seen as judgmental. I also try to never make it personal.

- You discipline those under your supervision in order to correct, to help, to improve—not to punish.

- Be slow to correct and quick to commend.

On Leadership

- Leadership is the ability to get individuals to work together for the common good and the best possible results while at the same time letting them know they did it themselves.

- A leader's most powerful ally is his or her own example.

- Knowledge alone is not enough to get desired results. You must have the more elusive ability to teach and to motivate. This defines a leader; if you can't teach and you can't motivate, you can't lead.

- Never be disagreeable just because you disagree.

- I was proud when Nellie [his wife] told an interviewer, "I never could tell whether John had a good practice or a bad practice, because he never brought it home."

- Profound responsibilities come with teaching and coaching. You can do so much good—or harm. It's why I believe that next to parenting, teaching and coaching are the two most important professions in the world.

We've looked at what's wrong with youth sports and have, with Coach Wooden's helpful wisdom, considered a better way. Now let's talk about some keys that I believe can lead to success in sports and life.

—Part 3—
The Keys to Success

7

The Coach Is Always Right–Even When He's Wrong

KEY #1: LEADERSHIP

Besides parents, we coaches are the earliest models of leadership kids have, so I can't emphasize enough the importance of what we say to them and how we say it, especially at young ages. A perfect example of how to do it right was caught on camera at the Little League World Series in Williamsport, Pennsylvania, last August.

It followed a dramatic elimination game in which an upstart team of underprivileged boys from Chicago, called Jackie Robinson West, jumped out to a four-run lead on the Cumberland, Rhode Island, Americans, later fell behind, then came back to win by a run.

That's a heartwarming story for the team from Chicago, of course, and they would go on to win the national championship and finish second in the world. But it was a gut-wrenching loss for the kids from Rhode Island. Their coach, Dave Belisle, immediately gathered them in shallow right field and knelt before them as tears streamed down their faces.

He said, "Everybody, heads up high. I've gotta see your eyes, guys. There's no disappointment in your effort, in the whole tournament, in the whole season. It's been an incredible journey.

"We fought. Look at the score—8-7, 12-10 in hits. We came to the last out. We didn't quit. That's us, boys, that's us!

"The only reason I'll probably end up shedding a tear is 'cause this is the last time I'm going to coach you guys. But I'm going to bring back with me, the coaching staff is going to bring back, you guys are going to bring back what no other team can but you guys—that's pride. Pride.

"You're going to have that for the rest of your lives, what you provided for the town of Cumberland. You had the whole place jumping, right? You had the whole state jumping. You had New England jumping. You had ESPN jumping.

"Want to know why? They like fighters. They like sportsmen. They like guys who don't quit. They like guys who play the game the right way. . . . We're one of the best teams in the world. Think about that for a second. In the world!

"So, we need to go see our parents, because they're so proud of you. One more thing. I want everyone to come in here for one big hug; then we're going to go celebrate. Then we're going to go back home to a big parade.

"I love you guys. I'm gonna love you forever. You've given me the most precious moment in my athletic and coaching career, and I've been coaching a long time—a *long* time. I need memories like this, I need kids like this. You're all my boys. You'll be the boys of summer.

"So, for the last time, we're gonna suck it up and we're going to yell 'Americans.' One, two, three—Americans!

"Okay, boys! Good job!"

That night on ESPN, Stephen Keener, president of Little League International, said Belisle was "one of the finest examples of a Little League coach I've ever seen."

IF I CAN remember more than thirty years later what Coach Golden said about me after a game one night, you *know* those kids will remember that encouragement for the rest of their lives, just as long as they will the sting of that loss.

Sometimes kids can be positively motivated by negative comments, but we coaches can never count on that, so we have to be very careful. That actually happened to me the summer after Coach Golden's seemingly rash statement gave me a glimpse of my possible future. But it sure could have gone the other way. Here's what happened:

It was the summer of 1984 and I was thirteen, in the middle of another season and looking forward to my freshman year at Reynoldsburg High School. Coach Golden, who was also quite a salesman, had his camps in full swing with one session of what he called his Baseball Instructional Service held at Franklin County Stadium, home of the AAA Clippers of the New York Yankees organization. The field baked in the summer sun, making the surface feel like a frying pan.

Those were some long days, but they exposed me to some of the best local talent, my age and above, and working with those kids improved my skills with me hardly even noticing.

Occasionally, Mr. Golden would ask a guest speaker to address the group—a local high school coach or some former college player. But this day he brought in a college coach to tell everybody what we needed to know about getting to the next level. He strutted onto the field in a full sweat suit bearing his school logo, and he looked pretty ridiculous pouring sweat in that blazing sun.

I could hardly breathe, but I sat there with my big, arrogant dreams of playing in the big leagues someday, thinking college might be just the stepping-stone I needed to get me there. Maybe this would be the guy who opened the door for me.

Just in case, I wanted him to see me sitting up straight and looking him directly in the eyes, just as my parents taught me. Well, he started rattling off statistics about how many players in Ohio and across the nation were every bit as talented as everyone he saw before him, how every one of them wanted to make the big leagues, and how astronomical were the odds against it. He said, "You might as well go out and buy a lottery ticket, because you've got a better chance of winning that."

Looking back on it now, I can't argue with his logic. He was encouraging us to be realistic and think first about getting our education—which makes a lot of sense and avoids a lot of crushed dreams.

But that's not the effect he had on me that day. All I could think was, *Who's this guy telling me I can't do this? Somebody has to make it, right? Why not me?*

I can still see that guy's flushed, sweating face and his terrible sweat suit. If he was trying to motivate me, it worked.

Be very careful what you say to kids.

That's not to say we coaches don't need to be realistic evaluators, too. There are times to step in and protect a kid who can't catch the ball or who simply doesn't have hand-eye coordination and needs to realize this is something that can't be taught. Just be careful that you're not the one who tells somebody they're never going to make it just because they're developing a little more slowly than most.

I would not want to have said something like that to Matt Carpenter, who didn't get drafted until the end of a red-shirted five-year stint at Texas Christian University and wound up getting only a thousand-dollar signing bonus from the Cardinals as their thirteenth-round pick in the 2009 draft.

He made his major-league debut two years later.

Slow to develop? Since then he has been a big-league all-star twice; become the first second baseman in Cardinals franchise history to win the Silver Slugger Award; led the major leagues in hits, runs scored, and doubles in 2013; and finished fourth in National League MVP balloting.

He's now our starting third baseman and leadoff hitter, and I can't tell you how thrilled I was for him when, in the middle of spring training last year, the Cardinals signed him to a six-year, $52 million extension through 2019, including an option for 2020 worth $18.5 million. Our general manager, John Mozeliak, cited his work ethic as a factor in the extension.

A big part of my job is to try to put each of our guys in positions where they can excel. The common goal is winning, and we're all clear on that. But we focus more on the team than on the individual. No one embodies that more than Matt.

Being drafted as a fifth-year senior means no professional team thought enough of him to even take a chance on him till then. He jumped into the deep end of a large pool of highly talented young prospects to see if he could swim. No life preserver, no second chances, just an opportunity. He worked and willed himself to get better every day, from one level to the next, until he was in the running for National League MVP in 2013, and now he's earned the life and career he always dreamed of.

I HAD LESSONS to learn on my own journey, lessons that affect how I see the whole issue of youth sports and that have shaped my own views on leadership to this day. One memory from my teen years sticks out.

I didn't turn fourteen until after I had started my freshman year in high school, and the following summer the kids on Ron Golden's traveling team were bigger and better than ever. I started thinking, *Man, these players are way better than me.* The positive motivation from Coach Golden and the negative motivation from that college coach kept me going for only so long. Baseball and life and puberty have a way of making a kid face himself eventually, and I started to seriously wonder what my odds were.

Added to that, the coach tried to make sure we were constantly pushed by making us play older teams. We had become known as a really good, very disciplined team, and we'd win a lot. People were coming out of the woodwork asking him, "Hey, would you take a look at my kid for your team?" We were playing so many older teams that he started bringing in a few older players, and he brought in a catcher who was bigger than I was. He was older by almost a year, and that year made a real difference.

I believed I was all-around a better player, but he was stronger, and it showed in how the ball came off his bat. Plus he had a better arm at that time.

After having caught all those games for all those years and having Coach Golden once say I was the best catcher in all of Ohio, suddenly being second string was entirely new for me. I was in a bad way and didn't know how to deal with it.

When I was a kid, there was no appeal process. If I got in trouble in school, the teacher was right and I was wrong, and any repercussions were doubled when I got home. The same was true in regard to my coaches. (I later learned that my parents were sometimes frustrated with my coaches and wanted desperately to say something in my defense, but they never did.)

Today, I believe too many parents feel an obligation to defend their children even when they're wrong. Believe me, I know the temptation. We all want to stick up for our kids. But what are we teaching them if we don't let them face their own difficulties? Life is tough, and people are going to mistreat them. We're not always going to be there to hold their hands.

One kid I grew up with had parents who would show up ready to fight his coach and threaten to take him off the team every time he was benched or disciplined. Eventually the coaches grew tired of it, and he was played less and less, even though he was talented. Not surprisingly, he didn't stay on teams long, and of course, he blamed it on the coaches.

Well, now it was my turn, and wow, I was miserable. I was riding the bench, and I was distraught, because all I ever wanted to do was to play.

My parents would drive me for hours to out-of-town tournaments just to watch me sit in the hot sun. On the way home, I'd be so mad I could hardly think, and I couldn't believe they didn't feel the same. I finally got up enough nerve to blurt, "I can't believe he's not playing me."

My parents' reply remains tattooed on my brain. It's as if they had rehearsed it. "Sometimes life isn't fair, but the coach is the coach, and he's always right, even when he's wrong."

What?

As you can imagine, that took some time to sink in. Emotion

always interferes with rational thinking. But once I got it, I got it. My job was to work even harder and make sure I gave my coach all the respect I possibly could.

Eventually I did, was soon back in the lineup, and there was no looking back.

The real kicker to that story came years later, in fact during my rookie season as a manager in 2012. The Cardinals were in the middle of interleague play against the Texas Rangers on June 23, and our ace, 6'6" Adam Wainwright, was on the mound. We were down a run in the sixth, and Waino was in a jam. I was determined that we finish the series strong and enjoy our off day before flying to Houston to face the Astros.

When I went to the mound to take him out, I saw that look in Adam's eye, and I knew he wasn't happy. No pitcher likes to be taken out, but usually they understand. Of course, I like a competitor who would rather stay in there, but my mind was on getting us out of the mess.

Anyway, the move didn't work out and the reliever allowed more runs, which led to a loss—for us and for Wainwright.

After the game, as always, I sat in front of the media, who picked apart every decision of the rookie manager nearing the end of his third month in the job. I tried to explain that I thought Adam had been working hard and had labored to get us to that point in the game.

As soon as the press finished with me, they had access to the players. One of the first questions to Adam was what he thought of his manager saying he "had labored." Stung by the loss and now having to wait four days for his next chance, Adam spoke his mind.

By the time I got back to my office, Waino wanted a closed-door conversation. He's one of the most competitive guys I've ever been around, and he was in the middle of a Cy Young–caliber season, so obviously he was not happy about having been taken out early. He was very respectful, but it took him a while to say everything he had on his mind.

When he finally finished I said, "Adam, I made a mistake. I made a decision, and it was the wrong one. I should have stayed with my ace longer, but I didn't, and it hurt us. I'm sorry for how it turned out, but my job is to do what I think is best for this team. Sometimes I'm wrong, and sometimes it hurts people. I followed my gut. I don't typically take my starter out when his pitch count is low and we still have a chance to catch up and he's not being forced out for a pinch hitter. But today I did, and now we're going to have to move forward."

We both felt good about the conversation, and as he's a hugger, we ended with a hug.

In Houston the next day, our media director, Brian Bartow, called to tell me of a newspaper story about dissension between Adam and me. The writer printed our respective quotes, but of course he didn't know about our private meeting. So while the story was accurate, it wasn't current.

A rift like that can be lethal to team chemistry. This had to be addressed, since we had more rookie players than any other team in baseball. They looked to veterans like Adam for how to conduct themselves as professionals.

I arrived early, as usual, to Minute Maid Park, and once again Waino was waiting for me. He said he was sorry for what was in the paper and wished he hadn't said anything. He also said he would talk with the young players and tell them how he should have handled the situation.

With the story having gained traction in the media on our off day the day before, I needed to say something to the team. As a rule, because of the length of the season, I don't have many team meetings, but this was important. I called everybody together and started by telling them I should never have taken our ace out of a game in that situation.

I said, "This wasn't my first mistake, and it won't be my last. I also want you to know that I realize that every decision I make somehow influences people in this room, and I take that very seriously. I want the best for the team, and I want the best for you individually. I do, however, have to make many quick decisions every game. Sometimes they work out, and other times they don't. Just understand that I'm trying to do what's best for all of us."

Then Adam asked if he could address the team. In front of them he apologized to me again for taking his frustrations to the media. He said he knew better and warned the young players that actions like that could tear a team apart. He also apologized to the team for letting them down and added that we all need to stand beside one another in good times and bad.

The lesson?

Always be willing to apologize. I witnessed a real man stand up and be a leader and make our team better. Adam wasn't saying he agreed with my decision, but he did understand something more important:

The coach is always right—even when he's wrong.

8

Let Your Catcher Call the Game

In the 1980s, we didn't have the technology we do today. Coach Golden was good about communicating with college coaches about prospects on his team before most other people were doing that kind of thing. I had had a really good summer before my junior year, and college and professional scouts started showing up. I didn't know where I wanted to go to school, but he advised me that it would be to my advantage to go to a place that really wanted me.

That seemed to make sense, and I was sure my parents would have some good advice. They always did. In fact, it wouldn't have surprised me if they had just told me which school I ought to go to. Having been raised the way I was, I wasn't what you would call the independent type. I hadn't been allowed to be. I was expected to do what I was told, and "Because I said so" had to be a good enough reason.

I don't remember ever asking my dad, "Why?" I wouldn't

have. My friends often gave me grief because I never questioned his authority, but I thank him to this day, because a lot of nonsense went on that I didn't need to be part of, and I'm glad I wasn't. So I was used to that kind of dynamic.

Maybe my parents overprotected me, but I didn't grow up in a bubble. Though my friends were into way more than they should have been, they never put pressure on me to join in. They knew what I believed, and they also knew I didn't want to make any decisions that would negatively affect my future. If the choice was a toss-up, they knew I was scared to death of my dad.

But when it came to talking to my parents about what college I should go to, I was in for the shock of my life. The kid who hadn't even had much say in what he wore to school every day was suddenly expected to make this decision by himself.

Dad's answer to "What should I do?": "You're on your own. Of course, you need to be praying about it. But this is something I don't know anything about. You're going to do this. You figure it out."

Maybe because my dad hadn't gone to college, the scholarship business was too far out of his comfort zone. When I could have used some real parental guidance, I had to navigate those waters alone. Part of me liked growing up and being independent, but when you're making big decisions at sixteen and seventeen, it can be scary. Even back in the late '80s, a full-ride scholarship to a major state university was worth a whole lot of money.

I started praying about it all the time.

I decided I wanted to go to the biggest school that would give me the best scholarship, and I started prioritizing them based on what they had to offer educationally. I took that very seriously.

That's something else I would urge you to carefully counsel

young athletes about. Because it's unlikely they'll play sports past their college years, they should choose their school based on academics first. What degree do you want to see on your wall for the rest of your life?

I was very interested in the University of Michigan. I didn't want to show my hand and say I wasn't interested in Ohio State, but I really wasn't because it was so close to home. Finally I considered offers from Nebraska, Michigan, kind of Ohio State, and Tennessee. I say "kind of" Ohio State, because there was another local catcher they had their eye on, and not only was he incredible, but he was also a grown man compared to me.

Going into my senior year I was 5'11" and 180 lbs. I don't know exactly how big he was, but I know he had first choice wherever he wanted to go. Every school I had an offer from, he was their choice. I didn't want to make the mistake of going to the same place he did and right away automatically become the number two freshman. So I just had to sit and wait to see what he did.

Finally the announcement came that he had signed his letter of intent to go to Ohio State, so that opened the door for me to go where I wanted, and I chose Michigan.

The Michigan coach did try to pull a switch on me when it came time to sign my letter of intent. With the press there and me all excited, he pulled out two letters and told me the new one would give him more freedom to sign other prospects, too. I thought that was dirty pool and chose to sign the one I had been promised. The next summer I would get another surprise.

By the end of my senior year in high school, lots of big-league scouts were blowing smoke, telling me I would be drafted really high, but no one really knew. Even at just seventeen, I had become pretty realistic. Unless I went in one of the early rounds, I planned to follow through with my commitment to Michigan, get my degree, see how baseball went there, and play it by ear from there.

Fortunately, whatever happened in the draft, I would be heading to South Dakota for much of the summer. I had been chosen for the North Team (representing Ohio, Michigan, Minnesota, Wisconsin, Illinois, and Indiana), one of the regional all-star prep squads at the Olympic Festival Games in Sioux Falls. We would then play other regional all-star teams with the goal of being chosen for the Junior USA Olympic team that would go on to play in Rapid City against international competition.

Since this was 1988, long before we all had phones in our pockets, during the draft I sat by the phone at home for two days. By then they were into rounds so low it didn't matter to me anymore. My dad and I grew so frustrated that we went and played golf, which was something I had never done with him before in my life. We both hacked so bad that we ran out of balls.

When we got home, he drove my little brother to one of his games, and wouldn't you know, the phone finally rang. It was the Toronto Blue Jays, apologizing because ". . . we forgot to call you, but congratulations, we drafted you."

"Wow, really? Thanks! What round?"

"Oh, that's not important, but you're now a member of our organization, so we'll be back to you soon with more details . . ."

I was excited just to have been acknowledged, but I also knew that my full-ride scholarship to a D-1 school was going to be worth a lot more than being drafted so late that one, the Blue Jays forgot to call me, and two, they didn't even have the heart to tell me which round.

At least I had a fun summer of good baseball to look forward to.

WHAT AN INCREDIBLE experience South Dakota became for me at such an age. I had a lot to learn and didn't even know it. Many of the guys I played with and against made it to at least the minors, and more than a handful made the big leagues. I learned I could hang with guys at that level, something I needed to know as I prepared to head off to Division 1 to fight for a starting position.

The Michigan coach had really flattered me, but with what happened the day I signed my letter of intent still on my mind, in South Dakota I also met one of my freshman teammates and contenders for the catcher's job. I knew I had my work cut out for me.

By the time I got home in mid-August, I'd actually almost forgotten about Toronto having drafted me. I mean, it was an honor, but I knew I couldn't have been quite what the pro teams were looking for, because I had gone in such a late round.

I visited the beautiful Michigan campus (which was bigger than Reynoldsburg), signed up for some classes, saw the legendary one-handed Jim Abbott pitch in Ray Fisher Stadium, packed with more than four thousand fans, and I was excited about becoming a Wolverine.

Once I found out who my roommate—another freshman ballplayer—was going to be, I contacted him and let him know that I wasn't into the party scene, wasn't a drinker and carouser and all that. He said, "That's a relief, man, 'cause neither am I." I was glad we had that established, because I had heard all the stories about college life.

I wasn't even thinking about the fact that until I would attend my first class several weeks later I was technically still the property of the Toronto Blue Jays.

Back home I went over to my high school with my best friend one morning to play some catch and have him throw me a little batting practice so I could stay sharp. When we got back to my house, the phone was ringing, and to my surprise, it was a representative from the Blue Jays. I didn't quite catch his name or his position, but he congratulated me on a good summer in South Dakota and asked if we could meet soon face-to-face. He said, "I'll be bringing Pat Gillick with me, and I'd like to know when would be convenient for you and your folks to meet with us there in your home so we can make you an offer."

He said Mr. Gillick's name as if I should've known who he was, and I should have (he was the general manager)—but I didn't. I quickly called my mother at work and we got the meeting scheduled, though I didn't really expect much from it. I had this idea it would be another local scout trying to convince my parents and me that I would become the next Johnny Bench.

While Dad and Mom were still very involved parents—he had sat by the phone with me during the draft, and Mom would be right there with him when two men from the Blue Jays showed up—I had a feeling this was another big decision I would be making on my own.

And I was right.

But then, I wasn't expecting much. Like I said, I hadn't really even paid attention to who was coming. I hadn't prepared for this meeting, and I hadn't prepared my parents for it either.

I recognized the voice of the man at the door as that of the man I had talked to on the phone. He introduced himself as Gord Ash, but I didn't know that name from the man in the moon. Then he said he was Toronto's assistant GM, and that got my attention. The man with him, Pat Gillick, had a presence. He also wore fancy cowboy boots, and when he sat in our living room, I realized he was a guy who could actually make decisions.

My mother offered lemonade all around as the men dripped sweat in our non-air-conditioned house and started negotiating right off the bat. They told me that even though they had drafted me so late—in a round so low they avoided even mentioning the number, their scouts noticed something in South Dakota that I had been unaware of.

Well, first off, I hadn't realized they had scouts in South Dakota. And what they had noticed was that I had shot up to 6'2".

Besides that, they liked my arm, my bat, my attitude, and the way I played enough that they said, "We're going to offer you close to second-round money." When they mentioned the figure, no one moved.

There I sat, just shy of my eighteenth birthday—in the presence of my dad, who knew what it meant to work seventy hours a week, and my mom, who scraped along on about the pay of a typical missionary—being offered a tick under six figures just to sign my name and agree to do what I'd always dreamed of doing.

Except for filling in on my brother's paper route once in a while, I had never worked a day in my life. And even then I was never paid.

Six figures is nothing to sneeze at today, and we're talking 1988. What in the world was going on? All of a sudden my decision had become a lot more complex.

I can look back now and see the strategy in Gillick and Ash's silence. They knew full well how that number sounded to this lower-middle-class family in the tiny house in the Columbus suburb. Nothing more needed to be said.

I finally looked at my parents and was met with blank stares.

Had they told me to get my education first, that would have been the end of it. Had they said I couldn't pass this up, that would have been my answer. Had they said we needed to discuss it, pray about it, think about it, whatever, that's what would have happened.

But again, I was on my own.

I do recall feeling pretty good about a professional team, especially one that had drafted me so late, now being eager to get me. And I wanted to act older than I was. I surprised myself by playing a little hardball, working to avoid showing that I had no idea what I was doing.

I stood and shook their hands and said, "Thank you. I think I need to go get my education."

"Very well," Mr. Ash said. "You take some time to think about it. You know, you're property of the Toronto Blue Jays until you go to your first class. So even if you get to campus and change your mind . . ."

Great, more to pray about. And I did a lot more of that, too.

Every couple of days between then and when I left for school, someone from the Blue Jays called to see if I'd changed my mind or had any questions or anything at all they could help me with. I assured them I'd let them know. One night one of my best friends stayed over, and the Blue Jays called early in the morning, suggesting they fly me to Toronto to see the dome, one of the wonders of the world.

I said, "Could my buddy come?"

They said, "Absolutely, and you can take batting practice with the team."

My friend was all jacked up, high-fiving me and saying, "You're not going to Michigan!"

But I knew better than to do that. Such a trip would have instantly negated my college eligibility. Yet even up to the day I left for Ann Arbor, I continued to get calls from the Blue Jays.

Even when I got to school, a few days before classes were to begin, they kept calling, upping the offer, reminding me I still had time as long as I hadn't gone to my first class. I was still feeling—and praying—my way through it. At one point I actually thought that if they got to a certain figure, I'd have to seriously consider it. I realize now how foolish that would have been, because I had no concept of how much would have immediately gone to income taxes. That would have made the decision easy.

At Michigan I was assigned to the East Quad dormitory with the rest of the baseball players. It felt good, jumping into a new environment and instantly being part of a team. At that time, *Baseball America* magazine was the bible for college sports, and they had the Michigan team ranked as having one of the best incoming freshman classes. We were all on the same floor and hung out together on and off the field and always had each other's back. We hadn't realized we had signed up for a full-time job with baseball, one that left little free time, but just being away from home meant a new level of freedom that was completely foreign to me.

One night, an upperclassman invited the freshmen to a party, and a lot of the baseball guys wanted to go. I grabbed my roommate, and we agreed we would go but steer clear of any trouble.

When we got there we found the party full of all the upperclassmen and people who liked to hang around the baseball team. Not long into it, the upperclassmen lined up the freshmen and announced it was time for shots. I was at the far end and my roommate was at the other, about third in line. As soon as they got to him he folded like a wet napkin and started throwing back drinks.

I was still seventeen, underage in any state, but I wasn't going to play that card. I simply wasn't a drinker and wasn't about to start then. But soon enough they made their way down to me. I said, "I'm not going to do it." Naturally everybody thought I was just trying to play tough guy and needed to be encouraged, so they all started laughing and cheering and shouting at me to drink my shots.

When I still refused, one of the upperclassmen got in my face and threatened me. I said, "Do what you gotta do, but I'm not doing it." I wasn't all that tough, but with two older brothers there wasn't much they could do to me that hadn't already been done.

Finally they dragged me outside, but rather than beating me up, they kicked me out of the party and sent me back to my dorm room. My drunk roommate was still upstairs with everybody else, so I had to leave by myself. The whole time I was walking back to the dorm, I was praying, "Is this how You're making my decision obvious?"

I'm passing up almost a hundred thousand for this? These are the guys I'm supposed to spend the next four years with and they send me home?

I was still sitting there stewing when my roommate finally got back and told me how sorry he was. Meanwhile, I was sure the whole team thought I was a total prude.

A few days later I awoke in time for my first class. Somehow, after all my praying, I still felt I was where I was supposed to be. The Blue Jays had told me to call them before I went to class, so I called Mr. Ash and said, "I appreciate the offer, and

I really did think hard about it. I just think I'm supposed to get my education."

He said, "You know, we really think you have a chance to make it and that your best chance is not to go to college but to go through the system. But we wish you all the best."

I cringe now to think of the kind of ballplayer I would have been for a big-league organization with my lack of maturity at seventeen. I clearly had some fortitude, but I was nowhere near ready. I still think about that today when I consider what to say to young ballplayers, whether on a youth-league team or kids breaking into the big leagues. Your talent can fool you into thinking you're way more mature than you really are.

At least I had finally made it official. If I were to ever play big-league baseball, I would have to be drafted again someday, hopefully having earned my way into an earlier round.

It felt good to have finally made the decision. I was excited. My future, at least for now, was set. I didn't have an extensive wardrobe, but I had bought myself a nice denim jacket and a cool book bag, and I had scheduled one of my easiest courses to start off with. I took a shower, got myself dressed, and confidently headed off to First Aid class.

As soon as I stepped outside, a pigeon the size of a turkey dropped its load right on top of my head. I mean, it covered my hair, my jacket, my book bag, everything. I could hardly believe it was real. At first I thought there was somebody on the roof pulling a prank on freshmen, but no, the smell convinced me.

By the time I got back to my room, showered again, changed clothes, and cleaned up my book bag, I was totally late. I hurried through empty corridors to my classroom, where they had already taken the roll and made introductions and were under way. I did happen to notice a gorgeous blonde in the first row. A little over four years later we would be married.

I HADN'T BEEN told there would be nine highly touted catchers at Michigan that season—my third unpleasant surprise. That made it all the more gratifying to win the job and be honored as Defensive Player of the Year at the end of the season.

The following year, former Detroit Tigers all-star Gold Glove catcher Bill Freehan was named the new head coach at Michigan, and Todd Winston, the kid I had met in South Dakota, and I would go head-to-head again for the starting catcher role.

Over the summer of '89, I played for legendary coach Joe Hayden on the Midland Redskins national champion Connie Mack team. Returning to Michigan in the fall at almost nineteen years old, I was eager to win the respect of a tough catching critic in Coach Freehan. I had no idea so much went into calling a game and handling a pitching staff. I had caught hundreds and hundreds of baseball games by then, but our teaching sessions seemed to be endless, and they often took place right in the middle of a game. I would be struggling to get my gear off and my batting helmet on, all while defending why I had chosen the pitches that I did.

Right off the bat I realized how fortunate I was to have a teammate like Todd Winston, a quality guy who loved to compete as much as I did. He wanted my job, and we even raced to the water fountain when it was time to get a drink! Every drill every day was a battle between the two of us, yet somehow we remained friends my whole time at Michigan.

I can say with certainty that there's no way I would have improved as much as I did without him pushing me like that every single day for three years. Todd was so talented that even though he didn't often get a chance to catch, he was eventually drafted as a catcher by the Houston Astros. It didn't surprise me either to learn that he went on to become a very successful high school coach.

What amazed me right from the start was how frustrated Bill Freehan was that my previous coach had called all the pitches. That coach had trained me like one of Pavlov's dogs to look to the dugout after every pitch. Finally Coach Freehan yelled, "Quit looking at me! Your pitcher is waiting for you to give him a good suggestion!"

That forever changed my philosophy on pitch-calling. If an all-star big-league catcher believes in using the guy behind the plate, why would anyone argue? If anyone had the credentials to call a game, it was Bill Freehan. But he knew doing that would not be the best for our team, and he also knew that would retard my growth as a potential professional catcher. It wasn't as if he didn't *want* to do the thinking. He spent so much time analyzing opposing hitters and teaching me how to get them out that he would have been the ideal pitch-caller.

Way too many youth, high school, and college coaches miss this important point. If you know how to call a great game from the bench, *don't do it.* Teach the guy who has the front-row view to do it.

I was fortunate that my youth-league baseball coach, Ron Golden, had been a catcher. A big part of my passion for the position came from the enjoyment I received from calling pitches. Learning to call the right pitch took some time, but he made it a point to have me think along with him to determine the right pitch in any given situation.

I admit the conversations with Coach Golden were not always warm and fuzzy, but there's a way to do the job properly behind the plate. There is not always a "perfect pitch" for every situation, but there is a thought process that must take place before telling your pitcher what to throw.

My first coach at Michigan had not had that philosophy. He had told me that college baseball was "too big a business" to risk a catcher making mistakes. He called the pitches, and I was to regurgitate whatever signal he sent from the dugout. I found myself losing concentration and growing bored behind the plate.

How was that possible? The catcher has so many responsibilities, but none as important as setting the tempo and helping control the pitching staff with pitch selection. Often I couldn't even remember what pitches certain hitters had hit against us, which was something that had always come second nature to me. There I was, a freshman in college, and I was on autopilot, going backward in my development.

Changing head coaches my sophomore year affected not only my college career but also the next two phases of my life, though this didn't become clear to me until later. Bill Freehan apparently saw something in me I hadn't seen myself, and he changed my way of thinking. One of the first things he told me was, "From now on, every elective class you have will be Spanish."

When I gave him a strange look, he laughed. He said he had already seen and heard enough to believe I had a chance to play professional baseball, and Spanish would prove invaluable for communicating to the growing Latin population of players. He later told me that he thought I would coach or manage someday and that Spanish would be a necessity. How's that for foresight? Spanish is the native language of some of my best players today, and while I don't claim to be fluent, I know it gives them a certain comfort level to know I understand them when they revert to it, especially in the heat of a game.

It's also a tremendous benefit to me when I'm dealing with a young player new to this country who is still struggling to learn English.

Then, I'll never forget when Coach Freehan told me that the catcher was the most important player on the field, and that if I couldn't think for myself and for the pitcher, I needed to find another position. He wanted the entire team to take our game to another level. "If calling the pitches from the bench is the way to win, every team in the big leagues would be doing it." The fact is, none of them do it.

We had impromptu pitch-calling classes whenever thoughts came to his mind, or whenever I had questions. I began to use my mind again, and I loved the challenge of trying to get it right and stay one step ahead of the opposition.

When I was drafted again in 1991 after my junior year and entered the minor-league system of the Milwaukee Brewers that summer at age twenty, one of the first questions the director of player development asked me was, "Did Bill Freehan call your pitches?" When I said no, he instantly knew he had a catcher who would be ahead of many of the others in the organization who had come from college and high school programs that didn't allow catchers to call the game.

Having the stamp of approval from a catching icon like Bill Freehan didn't hurt. Throughout the minors there was a premium on catchers who could handle a staff and had the ability to call pitches. I was happy to see the minor-league system had a plan in place for learning how to call a game.

Our big-league pitching coach, Don Rowe, spent hours on end with the minor-league pitchers and catchers in spring training. After a full day of workouts, Don would gather us in a hotel conference room almost every night, and class would begin.

I can't believe how much time that man invested into us young players, but his passion for pitch-calling hit a few of us right between the eyes. Skid, as everyone called him, had phrases and mental pictures for every sequence of pitches imaginable.

The beauty of his plan was that every pitcher, catcher, and manager could get on the same wavelength as to why a pitch was selected. More important, he reinforced the necessity to think behind the plate and to do what Bill Freehan challenged a group of collegiate athletes to do: think at a different level.

This was also borne out in my big-league career, right from the start. My first manager, the Milwaukee Brewers' Phil Garner, was a good baseball mind, and I truly enjoyed playing for him. My first regular-season start in 1994 was, naturally, a game I'll never forget. As I came off the field in the first inning, I was buzzing that I had actually started a game in the big leagues and was proudly making my way toward the far end of bench.

Gar grabbed me by the shoulder. "Hey, kid, what was the second pitch you threw to the second hitter?" He had caught me so off guard I couldn't even begin to think. "Don't ever call another pitch without a clear reason why you're calling it, and be ready to give me that reason when you come in here."

Though he never asked me like that again, you can bet your bottom dollar I had an answer for him. We had many discussions regarding pitch selection throughout the five seasons I played for him, but none as impactful as that first inning of my first game.

While playing for the St. Louis Cardinals from 2000 to 2004, the question I got most from our fans was related to my interaction with Hall of Fame manager Tony La Russa. Tony was so involved with every aspect of the game that people assumed he was calling pitches as well. It took me a couple of games to get into the routine Tony wanted, which was looking into the dugout after every pitch. He wanted to make sure he had my focus, in case he needed to change a defensive play or use me to communicate something to other players on the field.

I've never seen a manager who could handle so many things at once and never seem rushed or not prepared. The question from the media and fans alike was always, "Did Tony call that pitch?" when such-and-such happened. They obviously did not view me as honest, as they asked me that same question for years.

My answer was always, "No, the manager does not call the pitches. That is my job."

The only time I would look for help with pitch selection was when we had a big situation and a hitter was fouling off pitch after pitch and I was out of ideas. I would make eye contact with pitching coach Dave Duncan, basically asking, "Any ideas?" He'd either flash me a sign or just shrug. Even that happened only a handful of times over the years.

I hate to think we have somehow influenced youth-league coaches to call pitches from the bench, because I still have my catchers look into the dugout every pitch today. But there is no possible way I would ever be able to see from the dugout all the things my catchers can see. They are trained to look for adjustments in the batter's stance. Is he striding open, looking for the inside pitch? Has he moved closer to the plate, trying to take away the outside corner? Has he moved up in the box, looking for the breaking ball?

From the dugout we can't even tell if the previous pitch was inside, outside, or had any movement. All these things and more are almost unnoticeable except to a catcher's keen eye—and they work together to give your team a better chance of winning. That said, the heart of the matter in youth sports are the lessons along the way. From my experience in youth baseball, college, the minors, and now the majors, I'm convinced that if a coach can sit in the dugout and call pitches, then he should be able to teach the catcher to do the same for himself.

The risk is a few mistakes that may cost you a youth-level game.

The reward is helping a young player develop a passion for the catching position that he will carry for a lifetime.

Coach Freehan and the University of Michigan produced a lot of big-league baseball players, but the vast majority of the guys on Freehan's teams went on to other professions. I have to believe they took this same philosophy into other disciplines and workplaces, because really, at its core it's the epitome of knowing when and how to make confident decisions, and when to empower subordinates to make important ones for you.

9

Don't Think Less of Yourself, Think of Yourself Less

Key #3: Teamwork

Throughout my career, I've found that the organizations and coaches who emphasize winning at all costs win either only in the short run or not at all. But the ones who focus on the people, pursue perfection, strive for excellence, and emphasize getting the process right seem to also win the most over the long haul. They build great teams, and winning seems to follow.

The two most storied franchises in baseball history, in my opinion, are the Yankees and the Cardinals. They also have won the most World Series championships. Coincidence? I don't think so.

If the formula for success is so easy, why doesn't everyone follow it? The short answer is that it goes against human nature. Face it, most people enjoy the spotlight, taking the credit, being the star. But even the greatest stars in the history of, say, basketball, won their championships only when they learned to make their teammates better.

Magic Johnson.

Larry Bird.

Michael Jordan.

LeBron James.

Those four were superstars before they won championships. By themselves they couldn't carry their teams to titles. But when they also became ideal teammates, look what happened. During my days in the big leagues, I had the good fortune to play with teammates who taught me a lot more than baseball. They also taught me life lessons, which was a good thing, because I was eager to learn everything I could.

WHEN MY CAREER started to take off, I was trying to finish college, get married, and work my way up through the minors, so it was a good thing I had been raised by strict parents and coached for eight years as a kid by a man who believed in discipline. I knew what it meant to work hard and wasn't afraid of it. In the off-season I went back to Michigan to carry twenty hours of classes in '91 and twenty-one hours in '92, then completed an internship to graduate in December. The next month Kristin and I were married.

By the spring of 1994, when I was twenty-three, I was excited to be invited to spring training with the big-league club, because I had reached only AA ball by then and there were still several catchers ahead of me in the organization. I showed up in Phoenix not expecting much more than to get to meet some of my heroes and, hopefully, impress someone enough to get assigned to AAA when we broke camp.

We had an unusual spring, and our catchers began dropping

like flies to various injuries. All of a sudden, the skinny kid with number 98 on his back started getting some playing time. While just trying to do things right and keep my mouth shut, I played fairly well.

Because everyone else was hurt, I actually got to start one day against the Cubs. In the second inning, a Cubs batter charged the mound. Any self-respecting catcher knows his job in that situation is to protect his pitcher, so I raced out and got between them and even snuck in a couple of jabs.

I didn't think too much about it until after the game when our manager, Phil "Scrap Iron" Garner, was quoted: "I don't even know the name of the kid behind the plate, but he may have just made our ball club."

About a week later Phil called me into his office and sat, stogie in hand, studying me as I stared at him across his cluttered desk. He said, "Kid, I really don't want to do this, but you're going to have to make our team."

That wasn't exactly the way I had hoped to hear the words I'd dreamed of hearing all my life. He made it sound like they had tried everyone else on the planet and I was the last living soul left. It took a few seconds to register, but I left his office on cloud nine.

I went straight back to the team hotel, and it seemed like I dumped a hundred dollars' worth of quarters into the pay phone calling everybody I knew, and probably some I didn't, just to tell them I was going to the big leagues.

We had one last exhibition game, against the Tigers on April 1, before we opened the season. I caught a few innings and felt pretty good about hitting a double off David Wells. After the game, I was summoned to the manager's office, where a few veterans stood next to Garner's desk.

His face said it all. "I'm really sorry," he began, and I was afraid I was going to be sick right there. "It's my fault. I made a mistake. You do need some time in AAA before I can bring you up."

All I could think of was how many people I had told. I had been so close to my dream. What seemed an eternity of silence was all of a sudden a room full of laughter, and one of the guys yelled, "April Fools'!"

I didn't know whether to laugh, cry, or punch someone in the mouth. That was the meanest joke ever, but it made for a great story.

I sat and watched for most of April, with a pinch-hit at bat in a blowout and one pinch-catching appearance, where Gar brought me in to throw out a base stealer. I actually came running out of the bullpen as a defensive replacement in the ninth inning, the only time I've ever witnessed that move. Either way, I was part of an MLB team for the first time and couldn't have been more excited.

YOU DON'T HAVE to be a superstar to be a great teammate. A few I'll mention here have instantly recognizable names. Others may not be on the *Who's Who* list of baseball stars, but they made a tremendous impact on me because of how they played the game and how they conduct their lives. Each has something to teach us about teamwork.

ROBIN YOUNT AND Paul Molitor were both folk heroes to me as a young player coming up in the Milwaukee organization. They were already legends and clear future Hall of Famers, and I admit it's a stretch for me to even call them teammates, because we spent only part of one spring training together.

I was just another minor leaguer in the clubhouse, determined to be seen and not heard, and Molitor was a superstar who went out of his way to make a kid with one of those ridiculously high numbers on his back feel like part of the team. He didn't do anything specific or dramatic; he just talked to me, treated me like an equal, like a teammate. Believe me, that was uncommon. In thirteen years in the big leagues, I didn't see it often. More frequently, the stars didn't give no-name kids the time of day during spring training.

Robin Yount treated me the same way Paul Molitor did, and those random acts of kindness made a huge impression on me. I never became a superstar, but I learned how important it was to make scared rookies feel welcome and what a difference a veteran can make in a person's life just by treating him right.

I can't tell you how many times the memory of Molitor and Yount's kindnesses prompted me to tell our youth-league kids that their generation can help bring back the lost art of simply being kind. It's amazing how far this simple skill can take you and the impact it can have.

I'll never forget the team meeting at which the Brewers were to vote on whether to include coaches and trainers in the license-revenue sharing—the percentage given to the players for merchandise sold bearing the Major League Baseball Players Association logo.

The first voices raised in the clubhouse were angry, reminding everyone that "the fans come to see us play, and they buy merchandise because our name's on it."

I sank back into my locker, a player not yet out of the minors but still disgusted at the greed that emerged when the almighty dollar came into play. The players were going back and forth on the issue when Robin Yount stood, and the room immediately fell silent.

"You guys can do what you want," he said softly, "but I'm giving my portion to the coaches and trainers. These guys work longer hours than we do and make a fraction of the dollars. Every one of us in here makes good money and won't miss whatever is given to them. The dollars they get could change their lives."

Not another word was said, and the vote was unanimous to include the staff.

Thanks, Robin.

I've been fortunate enough to be in a couple of playoff-shares meetings since then, and I used that same message to help the people who deserved it.

My friend Derek Glanvill, president and chief operating officer at McCarthy Building Companies, Inc., is fond of quoting the maxim "The right thing is seldom the easy thing." Just like it couldn't have been easy for Robin to take a stand in that meeting, it won't be easy for our young players to face down peer pressure. But it will be the right thing.

KEVIN SEITZER WAS a big personality in the Milwaukee clubhouse, and was also one of the more vocal leaders. My lasting memory of Kevin is how he took a young catcher who barely made the team, gave him a place to stay, and looked after him on the road.

Kevin and I had many things in common, including our faith, and it made a big impression on me to see that a Christian could also compete like a wild man. His boldness in speaking out, though different from mine, was also encouraging. One of the character studies we conduct with our youth-team boys focuses on standing up for what you believe in. We emphasize that they don't need to force their opinions on others, but neither should they be afraid to defend their views, even when they aren't popular. We tell them that their teammates will respect and appreciate that, even if they won't admit it in front of others.

Kevin was also a stickler for playing the game the right way, treating teammates with respect, and looking for ways to specifically encourage a different person every day.

Those traits extended beyond his playing days, and he became a successful big-league hitting coach and now runs a top-tier youth-baseball training organization known as Mac-N-Seitz.

CAL ELDRED, THE ace of the staff on my first big-league team, was the epitome of a competitor, which made him the most respected young player I had ever been around. He had a tough demeanor on the mound, even before he had spent much time in the big leagues. I mean he was not afraid of anyone or any situation. I was also impressed that while he was a godly man of faith, he wasn't afraid to fight for his teammates and for what he believed in. Too often, as I'll discuss in the next chapter, Christian athletes are criticized for being meek. I think it's important that we show class and are above reproach, but I often talked to the youth-league boys about Cal, because he was an example of a man who didn't shy away from being a man. He knew what he stood for and he knew what he would fight for, and that's the very definition of a man with authority.

PAUL QUANTRILL, A pitcher I caught only briefly in Toronto in 1999, was one of the toughest players I ever worked with, and he probably got more out of his ability than anyone. Q played for seven different teams during his fifteen-year big-league career. While he never had overpowering stuff, he relied on pinpoint control and a ferocious desire to win.

I list Paul as an ideal teammate because he was one who made a conscious effort every day to make the people around him better. He was always positive but never afraid to tell a teammate the truth if he thought they weren't competing at the level he thought they should. He was selfless, fiery, and incredibly disciplined in his dedication to his craft.

MARK MCGWIRE WAS a great player, a great guy, and a great teammate.

The baseball player strike of 1994 left fans feeling hurt, and the healing process was slow. The great home-run race between Mark McGwire of the Cardinals and Sammy Sosa of the Cubs a few seasons later went a long way toward bringing back the excitement and the crowds. The steroid controversy that came later may have left a bad taste in a lot of people's mouths, but there was no denying the drama of 1998.

Unfortunately for me and the Brewers, I had one of the worst seats for that epic battle, because our club had committed to challenging those guys, and they both made us pay. While lots of other teams may have decided to try to pitch around them, we decided to go right after them, strength against strength.

It turned out to be an incredible, and needed, season for the game. In my opinion, Mark was one of the key factors in getting the game back on its feet and to the strong state we see it in today. I'm also proud to list him as one of my ideal teammates, because I got a chance to play with him in St. Louis in 2000 and 2001.

I learned something every time I ate a meal with Mark and watched how he interacted with fans. Most of us players could mix into a crowd fairly easily, but not so with him. That guy looks like a comic book hero, and people couldn't help but notice. Even when it wasn't convenient, Mark would take time to talk with kids, and he always treated people with respect—even when he knew it was someone just trying to make a buck off his autograph.

He was always kind to my kids, too, and even they couldn't help but stare at him. I would insist they call him Mr. McGwire, and he would say, "Hey, I'm bigger than your dad, and my name is Mark."

I'd say, "Yeah, but you kids are going home with me, and his name is 'Mr. McGwire.'"

Though many criticized Mark for his testimony before Congress regarding performance-enhancing drugs, I was proud to tell the young boys I coached that I applauded his honesty and remorse. Even our heroes sometimes do things we don't understand. Bob Humphreys, the first director of player development I ever played under, liked to remind us, "Boys, it takes years to build a good reputation and one second to lose it."

Pat Hentgen made a lasting impression on me of what a staff ace should do and how his efforts can multiply over time. Pat spent a lot of his free time with Roy Halladay and Chris Carpenter, two young pitchers nobody really knew, though they seemed to have bright futures. Pat spent time with them on and off the field talking shop, a fading art in the game now.

The wisdom of a veteran player is best shared during a game or right after, when thoughts are fresh. Most important, Pat watched the game through the eyes of a learner, teaching future stars and innocent bystanders how good players become great: through hard work and a relentless pursuit of a competitive edge.

I also have a soft spot for Pat because his recommendation to Tony La Russa after the 1999 season led Tony to invite me to spring training with the Cards. Pat was a top-shelf competitor and teammate. The Phillies and Cardinals, after their most recent World Series championships, owe him thank-you notes for his example, which is being passed on to the next generation.

SHAWON DUNSTON AND Eric Davis were a pair of all-star-caliber veterans who wound up in St. Louis in 2000 at the ends of their careers and found themselves in backup roles. This happens to everyone, and often such players are bitter about their careers coming to a close and grow sullen, barking out orders to the younger players or sitting at the end of the bench like the two old Muppets in the balcony, making snide remarks about every play that doesn't go well.

But not Shawon and Eric. Those guys understood the responsibility of leadership and had bigger roles in mind for themselves. The reputations they had built over the years allowed them to say what needed to be said, whether to a twenty-one-year-old rookie or a fifteen-year veteran. Shawon would even call out Mark McGwire if he deserved it, and Mark would take it.

What impressed me, too, was that everything Shawon and Eric said and did reinforced the team concept. I'm convinced it was their attitudes and energy as much as anything that helped get the most out of everyone and get us to the playoffs that season.

YANKEES MANAGER JOE Girardi was briefly a teammate of mine in 2003 at St. Louis. I've always had the utmost respect for how he went about his business as a player and as a manager. He has exemplified consistency and balance while occupying what I consider the hottest seat in organized sports.

Joe reached out to me when I became manager of the Cardinals. He offered great advice on things he had learned as a young manager and then handed the phone to his wife so I could get some insight on how to handle the challenges of having a young family while managing.

Albert Pujols makes my list because he was the most focused player I have ever seen. His intensity before a game could offend the media and even some of his teammates who didn't understand that he simply would not be bothered, but the fact is he spends April through October thinking every day about what pitcher he's going to make pay. Over the course of 162 games, I never saw him give away an at bat. If Albert had four hits, he approached the fifth at bat as if his next meal depended on it.

I never really had to teach our youth-baseball team about Albert, because they got to witness it firsthand. Imagine you're a kid at an indoor practice facility when your coach sits you down and tells you he has someone who wants to talk hitting with you for a few minutes, and then Albert Pujols walks in.

The boys' jaws dropped to the floor. And he wasn't just passing time. He truly wanted to help them get better. He would stay and work with the boys individually, and a few weeks later he might show up again and work with the infielders or just say a few words to the team. It was priceless.

I'm one of the fortunate few who were able to spend time with him in the off-season and also got to see the humanitarian who cares for so many people.

A rare talent with a huge heart.

JOHN MABRY, A teammate in St. Louis and now our hitting coach, was my longtime workout partner and probably helped me stay in the league by constantly helping me with my terrible swing and agreeing to new, crazy workouts every winter. He's one of the most loyal people I have ever met, with one of the best reputations of any player who has walked through the doors of the clubhouse. That's a good friend.

DARRYL KILE WAS one of my all-time favorites because of his selflessness. He told me he would pick out somebody to specifically encourage every day, other than the day before and the day he pitched. Those days he was all business, and like most pitchers, he had a one-track mind.

But those other three days, Darryl would go out of his way to do things for someone and boost the guy's confidence. After I became aware of this practice, I could tell when it was me, and I'd say, "I'm your guy today, aren't I?" He'd just look at me and laugh.

When Darryl suddenly died of a heart attack in his hotel room in June of 2002 at age thirty-three, it was my darkest day in baseball. I lost one of my dearest friends.

KIRK RUETER OF the Giants was a great teammate, even though I barely knew him. When my grandfather passed away during the 2005 season, Kirk quickly scheduled a private plane to fly my family and me to West Virginia in time for the funeral. That act of kindness wasn't just a one-time thing but was representative of his day-to-day efforts to make everyone around him better.

————

If there was one thing I learned early, it was how teammates ought to treat one another. My youth-league coaches, including my dad and Ron Golden, had trained me well in this, but I got a real lesson in it that first full season in professional ball. It forever solidified with me that the Golden Rule applies to a baseball team as importantly as anywhere else. My pet peeve to this day is a player not treating a teammate the way he would want to be treated, and that often requires a healthy dose of tough love—in other words, confrontation.

I hope I'm developing a reputation as a pretty even-minded manager, which is the way I like it. But if you want to push my buttons and set me off, show up a teammate. You'll see a side of me you might wish you hadn't. I simply will not tolerate a player displaying any outward sign of disapproval of or frustration with a teammate. I tell my big-league guys there is never a reason good enough to justify that.

For example, if one of our pitchers wants to see me snap, all he has to do is flap his arms in frustration when an infielder misplays a ground ball. Our guys spend so much time trying to hone their craft, they want nothing more than to make every play. Nobody makes an error on purpose. Inevitably, someone will forget and show up a teammate, and I'll have to have "the talk" with him. This is a big deal if you want to have harmony in your clubhouse—or a youth-league dugout.

It happened to me in 1992, during my first full pro season when I was a twenty-one-year-old catching a more experienced pitcher one night, and we were clearly not on the same page. He kept shaking off pitches and making it obvious he was frustrated with my pitch-calling. We were losing, he was taking it out on the guy behind the plate, and everyone in the stadium could see it. I was ticked, but I didn't know how to handle it.

After the game, my manager, Tim Ireland, screamed for me to get in his office, and he let me have it for letting my pitcher stand out there and embarrass me, himself, and our squad. "You march out there and find him right now and tell him if he ever does that again, you'll fight him right on the mound!"

I was good at doing what I was told, but I couldn't find him. Finally, someone told me he was on the toilet, and I knew he couldn't get away from me there. I forced the door open and read him the riot act while he sat there! Needless to say, no one showed up anyone else the rest of that year. Tim Ireland knew the message needed to come from a player that showing up a teammate would not be tolerated.

Coincidentally, the same thing happened my first year in spring training with the Brewers, before I made the big-league club in 1994. Phil Garner put me in a very similar situation, knowing well before I did that I had a chance to make the team. Looking back, I can see he wanted to make sure I could handle the leadership responsibilities required by a catcher.

A veteran starting his ninth big-league season was frustrated with the snot-nosed twenty-three-year-old behind the plate, and he displayed some obvious reaction every time I failed to call the pitch he wanted. Finally he threw up his hands and waved me out to the mound, making it clear to everyone that he was not happy with me.

I got through the game, but the whole time I was thinking about Tim Ireland and the message I would have given that pitcher had we been equals on a minor-league team. But this was a decorated big-league veteran and I was an AA wannabe.

After the game, Gar called me in, and as Yogi Berra was famous for saying, it was déjà vu all over again. He didn't yell as

Ireland had, but the message was the same. He said, "Kid, when you're trying to help a guy and he shows you up like that, you need to do something about it. If you don't stop it now, it'll never end. Don't embarrass him in front of his teammates, but somewhere away from the field tell him if he ever does that again, you're gonna kick the tar out of him."

I really didn't want to do it this time, but I had no choice. I worked up enough nerve to knock on his hotel room door and stumble through my rehearsed lines, shaking the whole time. To my surprise, he apologized.

When it comes to kids, obviously I would not encourage them to threaten the offender. But I would urge them to tell the other player how it made them feel. I would then talk to the team and reemphasize the importance of being a good teammate. That starts and ends with thinking more about your team than you do about yourself. Selflessness is the goal—not thinking less of yourself, but thinking of yourself less.

Make no mistake, developing that mind-set is not easy. It's opposed by our culture and every fiber of our being. Instinct and billions of dollars in marketing tell kids to get what they can when they can, and do whatever they have to do to get it. But any team that allows selfishness to permeate its structure will fail. We encourage the boys to figure out how to make everyone around them better, and our job as coaches is to exemplify this. That means not overreacting to mistakes, which will happen often. If the boys see us encourage in public and correct in private, they keep their dignity and the example is set.

ONE OF THE first things I try to impress upon young players, whether at the youth level or in the big leagues, is what I expect from them. It begins with respect. In spring training with the Cardinals, I make it clear that we treat people in our clubhouse—regardless of their role or position—like family. We are all part of something bigger. I encourage young players to never fall into the trap of believing they have somehow earned the right to treat anyone as if they are beneath them.

This happens to be one of those biblical values that never go out of style. Value others over yourself and practice the Golden Rule, and you'll find harmony in your marriage, your family, your workplace, everywhere. Some truths are just universal, and this is one.

Talent can take a player a long way in this game. But if we start believing our press or thinking we're something special because we've been lucky enough to be gifted with outstanding athletic ability, we are setting ourselves up for failure. What makes us think we're better than someone else who may have abilities in some other area that just don't get as much attention? Maybe you can hit a ball four hundred feet and throw a runner out on the fly from the warning track. Can you overhaul an engine or handcraft a kitchen cabinet or teach school all day?

I also like to impress upon the players the importance of becoming a good listener. I direct this toward younger players so they don't miss the opportunity to hear from veterans and coaches. But this is a challenge to all of us, myself included, to work on things that will help us in our careers and in all areas of our lives.

I don't claim to have it all figured out. I try to cover areas I want to improve in as well. I challenge young players to be silent and respectful of the older players, and for veterans to truly listen to the questions and concerns of the younger guys. Listening skills can be applied to every relationship.

It can become a cancer in the clubhouse when young players would rather talk than listen, and come in acting—and
talking—as if they already know it all. The veterans usually
grant them their wish and avoid them; then the kids have no one
to turn to when things go bad—which they *always* do at one time
or another over the course of 162 games—and they need advice.
But the kids who come in quiet and eager to learn find they get
all the attention and input they can handle.

Another crucial component of a great team atmosphere is
a quote attributed to the former Chairman of the Joint Chiefs
of Staff, General Colin Powell: "Perpetual optimism is a force
multiplier."

That sounds fairly simple, but I've found it powerful. My
rookie year as manager in 2012, I faced the pressure of having
inherited the defending World Series champions from Tony
La Russa—one of the most popular and legendary Cardinals
managers ever (no pressure there). I knew going in, of course,
that I would not have the most potent offensive weapon in baseball for the last decade—Albert Pujols—who had jumped to the
American League. But we had also lost four other key players, at
least temporarily.

Our guys could easily have used these losses as excuses. I
could have, too. Naysayers could have pointed to all this—not to
mention the brand-new manager—and predict nothing but woe.
As you can imagine, that wasn't my mind-set. And to my great
encouragement, that wasn't true of my guys either.

Every once in a while you find a group that seems to stand
taller and straighter the tougher things get. They stick out their
chin and say, "Okay, bring it on." I loved the fight in those guys
and the fact that they couldn't wait to prove people wrong.

For the record, we had enough issues that spring and sure

weren't looking for more. But I do know perpetual optimism became part of our DNA and played a huge role in taking us to the playoffs.

A third concept that extends far beyond baseball and sports in general is the importance of a talent the rest of your people can follow. When the Cardinals were able to work out a deal with our ace, Adam Wainwright, in the spring of 2013, I told the media that the value of a pitcher like him went way beyond wins and losses. It was crucial to have a leader like Adam in place to show our many aspiring big leaguers how to go about their business, on and off the field, with class.

From a baseball perspective, Adam brought a versatile résumé to the plate that not many players could match. He had been a Cy Young–caliber starter and a closer who had finished out a World Series championship in 2006, plus he had come through Tommy John ligament-replacement surgery. Here was a pitcher with the ability to speak to many players on our club, guiding them by sharing his firsthand experience.

Not only is Adam a leader in the clubhouse and in the community, he's a fierce competitor who also keeps his teammates loose when he's not pitching. The guys admire and respect him as a pitcher and a person.

What a gift to manage a team that has a true leader in every corner of the clubhouse. Besides Adam, I'm blessed with Yadier Molina, in my opinion the best catcher on the planet. Yadi and I were both influenced by the late legendary catching instructor Dave Ricketts. Yadi learned so much under Dave, but probably nothing more important than proving your respect for the game by how hard you prepare and play and by demanding the same from your pitching staff and teammates.

Matt Holliday is a quiet force who doesn't get up in front of the team and give big speeches, but rather leads by example. The way he shows up every day, works relentlessly, and is ready to play regardless of how he feels or what happened the night before says more than words ever could.

It's an incredible gift for a coach or manager to have his most talented players also be his most disciplined. A goal of every coach should be to get his most advanced players to be the ones pushing the hardest. Their constant striving to be better sets the tone for the rest of the team. A coach at any level can only do so much if his best players are not doing the things he needs the rest of the team to do. They are the engines that drive the train.

I make it a point to tell my guys each season that we walk into spring training as a group of sixty individuals with no guarantee that we'll develop into a team. Becoming a team is anything but automatic. It's the result of a lot of hard work, and it only begins to take shape when we start looking out for one another. You can imagine how hard that is when one of the primary goals of spring training is to get from sixty players to twenty-five for opening day. How does a kid with a big-league dream look out for everybody else when he's trying to stand out and impress enough to be one of the twenty-five survivors?

Ironically, by proving he can be a team player. It's not easy.

Every spring we face unique challenges that mirror the ones everyone faces in life: priorities and how you balance them. Every such decision is an opportunity to grow. Family issues come up, and you have to make tough calls. Even veterans face the choice: tend to their families or stay with the team? The right thing is almost always to put their families first, but that usually puts the team in a tough spot. The same is true in your life. Doing the right thing at home may be the worst thing you can do at the office or in your career or in your social circle.

In our case, we play such a long season that it's inevitable that things come up in the home lives of our players. This is also an issue with many youth teams, and frankly, I see mistakes made by coaches at that level all the time. I understand it takes commitment to make a good team run, but many coaches don't leave families any room to enjoy their summers aside from the baseball schedule.

Try to remember that these kids have these summer breaks for only a few years, and this is when they can create lifelong memories with their families. Try stocking your team with some alternate players who can fill in when necessary, and ask parents to lay out their summer plans early, so you can schedule tournaments and games around the dates that multiple families will be gone. It will help you keep a team's priorities straight, and it's easier than you think.

10

Stand Your Ground

KEY #4: FAITH

> I have no hidden agenda, no ulterior motives. My priorities in life will permeate how I coach and what I expect from the boys. My Christian faith guides my life, and while I have never been one to force it down someone's throat, I also believe it's cowardly and hypocritical to shy away from what I believe. You parents need to know that when the opportunity presents itself, I will be honest about what I believe. That may make some uncomfortable, but I did that as a player, and I want it out in the open from the beginning that I plan to continue it now.
>
> —FROM MY ORIGINAL LETTER

You may be cringing now, and I completely understand. We don't talk about matters of faith as freely as we once did; however, I am, without apology, a Christian. With that comes an obligation, a responsibility to live up to who I say I am—or, more precisely, Whose I say I am.

I have a responsibility not to be ashamed, even if it has become clear that it is no longer politically correct to be vocal about one's faith. The question becomes how to live out my beliefs in the job I now find myself in. At the time I wrote the proclamation above, I was staking ground in a fairly confined arena—one youth-league baseball team, if they would have me.

Since then, I have been thrust into a position much more public than I ever anticipated, where each day tests my resolve and commitment. Do I still mean what I say when the whole world is watching?

We all know people who wear their emotions, passions, political leanings, social views, and religious beliefs on their sleeves for everyone to see, whether or not anyone is interested. While I may admire their boldness, I am simply not that type of person. I have committed to my players and coaches that I will never force my faith down their throats or assume they see the world as I see it; however, neither will I cower from any question.

I consider it a high honor to walk through life with the men I am entrusted to coach. Life is not always fair, and troubles are unavoidable. If I do my job the way I believe I should, conversations are bound to come up that go deeper than batting slumps and sore shoulders. If during such a conversation I have the opportunity to share from personal experience, and my experience happens to include my relationship with God, I will share that without hesitation.

My goal is to live in such a way that what I believe is obvious by how I go about my business and how I treat others.

I WAS RAISED in a Christian home, but an old saying puts that in perspective: being born in a Christian family doesn't make you a Christian, any more than being born in a garage makes you a car. I had to come to faith on my own, and then I had to come to own my faith. Most people who become believers at young ages, as I did, come to a point later when they have to face whether they just inherited a belief system from their parents or really accepted it for themselves.

Here's how it happened with me:

I've told you how my parents had my brothers and me in church just about any time the doors were open. So when I was a kid I fell into a trap that a lot of people do. I became religious, which may not sound so bad. In fact, you may wonder, well, isn't that the goal? I think that's what I thought. I grew so comfortable with the routine, I knew every nook and cranny of that church and places to hide. Not only did I know every part of the service, but I also knew almost every song without having to open the hymn book.

Then one summer when I was about ten our church held a revival in a tent outside and brought in a Southern Baptist preacher. My best friend and I picked out our spots on a bench near the back where we sat every night.

Well, I thought this preacher was whacked out up there at the pulpit, pounding his Bible and making a lot more noise than I normally heard at church. At least he got my attention. By that age I had memorized a lot of Bible verses and knew all the stories. Like I said, I was pretty religious.

But this guy began calling out us churchgoers, demanding to know, "Who is Jesus Christ to you? Who is He to you personally? I don't care about your résumé or your pedigree or what your parents do!"

And I swear, it was like he was looking right at me, to the point where I was thinking, *Cut it out, man!* Now, some people, when they have that experience, feel as if they've come "under conviction," a feeling of deep guilt over their sin. I didn't feel that at all. I was just insulted!

He kept pounding the questions, and I kept thinking, *Man, you don't get it! You're talking to the same people who are in church here every week. We know this stuff.*

But he kept saying, "I'm talking to you! If you don't think I'm talking to you, yet you don't know personally who this Jesus Christ is, you're missing it." He was making the case that religion is *not* the point. If you research Jesus's life even a little, you'll find that religious people were the ones He had the most trouble with. Religion is people's idea of how to reach God. Jesus is God's idea of how to reach people.

I'd spent as much time in church as I did on the ball field, so I had been in the right place physically, but now this preacher had me wondering. Did I personally know who Jesus was? Who was He to me? Had I given Him my heart?

"You need to make a decision for yourself as to who Jesus Christ is for you," he thundered, and all of a sudden I sensed I might need to make a change. Maybe I wasn't under conviction, but man, did God grab me by the scruff of the neck that night. If nothing else, I was deeply puzzled. All the way home I wrestled with this. The wheels were really turning, and even at bedtime my mind was still racing.

I asked my older brother in the bunk above, "What do you think about what that preacher said? Could we be missing it?"

"No. Shut up."

I peppered him with questions, like if it could be true that knowing Jesus for yourself had nothing to do with your parents or being religious. He finally said, "Enough! Be quiet!"

"Yeah, but what about what he said about people who've been going to church all their lives like we have, and—?"

"Mike! Go to sleep!"

"But if it's possible that I've been—"

"If you say one more word—"

If there was one firm rule in our house, it was that we were not to get out of bed before morning. As a parent now I can sure see why they had to enforce that in a house that small. But I had to talk to Mom and Dad. There was no way I could sleep with all that was going on in my head.

I know I'm gonna get in trouble, I thought, having no idea that answering such questions would be the greatest thrill for any Christian parents. I finally worked up the courage and padded out to the living room and then just laid out all the things I had asked my brother.

Immediately their faces lit up. They got out their Bible, opened it to the New Testament book of Romans, and walked me through its Road to Salvation:

The Romans Road to Salvation
(Verses from the New Living Translation)

1. Who needs it?

"For everyone has sinned; we all fall short of God's glorious standard." (Romans 3:23)

2. Why we need it.

"For the wages of sin is death . . ." (Romans 6:23a)

3. How God provides it.

"But God showed his great love for us by sending Christ to die for us while we were still sinners." (Romans 5:8)

4. How we receive it.

". . . but the free gift of God is eternal life through Christ Jesus our Lord." (Romans 6:23b)

5. The results of it and how we're assured of it.

"Well then, should we keep on sinning so that God can show us more and more of his wonderful grace? Of course not! Since we have died to sin, how can we continue to live in it? Or have you forgotten that when we were joined with Christ Jesus in baptism, we joined him in his death? For we died and were buried with Christ by baptism. And just as Christ was raised from the dead by the glorious power of the Father, now we also may live new lives." (Romans 6:1–4)

"If you openly declare that Jesus is Lord and believe in your heart that God raised him from the dead, you will be saved. For it is by believing in your heart that you are made right with God, and it is by openly declaring your faith that you are saved." (Romans 10:9–10)

"For 'Everyone who calls on the name of the Lord will be saved.'" (Romans 10:13)

Then they prayed with me, and I received Christ.

I WENT THROUGH a lot of years when I was what I would call a closet Christian. I wasn't ashamed of my faith; I just wasn't outspoken about it. Once I got into high school, I got involved in the Fellowship of Christian Athletes (FCA). That—and the fear of my dad—kept me on the straight and narrow, but I have to say I always had an uncanny sense of where God wanted me to be and an awareness of the things I shouldn't be doing.

It wasn't easy, either, because our school was rough. At one point a national magazine ranked our school number three in the country for drug use and number one for teen pregnancy. Those were hardly badges of honor for a high school in a middle-class suburb of Columbus, but when our principal called an assembly to announce and discuss those sad statistics, the whole place seemed to erupt like it was some great accomplishment.

I'm sure I often came off proud to the point of self-righteous about avoiding that whole scene, but I remain grateful to this day that I held certain convictions and didn't get into things I would live to regret. I confess I did have to learn to become less judgmental and not so much of a know-it-all, especially when it came to people of other faiths and persuasions—particularly those of just a slightly different stripe than my own.

Believing you have all the answers can put you in a dangerous spot, because it leads you to think that everyone ought to see everything the way you do. Even my own wife was raised in a different tradition, and for way too long I considered it my mission to educate her on such matters. How the young, naïve version of Mike Matheny didn't totally offend and alienate her and her family I still don't know. But they're forgiving and understanding, and you live, you learn, you grow.

It probably wasn't until my first season in pro ball that I began to get the picture of how narrow my view had been of what it meant to be a true believer in Christ. And I also realized how casual I had been about sharing my faith.

When I was drafted by Milwaukee following my junior year at Michigan, I was assigned to rookie ball in Helena, Montana, and our first game happened to fall on a Sunday. A bunch of us brand-new guys showed up, knowing nothing of the routine and thinking that it was pretty cool to be ballplayers who were finally getting paid to play. While we were getting our uniforms on, a nicely dressed guy came in carrying a briefcase and said, "We've got chapel in five minutes in the bleachers."

When he walked out we all looked at one another. He hadn't said he was with the Brewers or if chapel was optional or what. So pretty much the whole team went out and sat in the bleachers. When the guy started chapel, we knew immediately he wasn't with the organization. We also knew he meant business. He didn't hold back.

"As a guy who loves baseball," he began, "this is intimidating for me. I'd love to say I'm as talented as you guys, try and puff myself up and tell stories about how good I used to be or how good I still could be. Even if that were true, it would be a complete waste of your time. Here's all I want you to know. It doesn't matter if you remember anything about me. If you were to die today without knowing Jesus Christ as your Savior, you'd spend an eternity separated from Him . . ."

Clearly there were guys who were offended by this man's bluntness. Maybe they thought he was going to say something inspirational that would help them get four hits that day or throw a shutout. But he just fired the truth right at them. Something about it really resonated with me.

I had heard chapel speakers before, and they did all seem to have to fight the temptation to try to impress the players with their own sports backgrounds. This guy made it all about the message and not about himself. As soon as I got the chance I told him that I, too, was a Christian and that I thought he had just nailed it.

We soon became friends.

What I found cool about that summer was that at one point I looked over the field and realized that just through the consistent love and servant nature of this volunteer chaplain, nine players had come to faith in Christ.

As awesome as that was, I have to admit that he also started calling me out. He said, "Mike, you know everything there is to know about all this, but you've been turtling up and hiding it."

I got defensive. I said, "I'm not hiding it. I'm just not throwing it in everybody's face."

"Fine. What *are* you doing with it?"

What could I say? He was right. I began looking for more opportunities to talk about my faith, but that, too, was when I needed to learn sensitivity and grace. As I worked my way up through the minor-league system, I became exposed to more people from different walks of life and was taught to become more relational.

I learned a lot from one of my coaches, Chris Bando, who was very devout in his faith. Chris was my AAA manager in New Orleans when I got sent down from the Brewers just before the major-league strike in 1994, and then he was my catching coach in the big leagues for the rest of my time in Milwaukee. He kept his priorities straight, once saying, "Good things can become bad things when they keep you from the best things."

Any maturity I gained in the area of sensitivity came when Kristin and I moved to St. Louis after we married in January of 1993. I needed a place to work out and got connected with some of the Cardinals. One invited me to a Bible study taught by a man named Walt Enoch, one of the original staff members of the local FCA ministry. I was intimidated by the group, which included many big leaguers and other professional athletes, among others—so I didn't say much.

But that's where I began to learn how naïve I had been about some of the things I had said to my wife and my in-laws and many others over the years. Just watching Walt and hearing him interact with people was a lesson in how to lovingly communicate. The way he expressed himself without offending is something I've rarely seen since. He taught me to be unapologetic as a believer but to also walk that fine line between boldness and putting people off.

IT'S NOT ALWAYS easy to follow Walt's example, though, and I know that many Christian athletes and coaches struggle with language problems. They confuse meekness with weakness, and salty language seems to go hand-in-hand with being a fiery player or leader. I admit there are lots of times when I'm addressing my team or arguing with an umpire that it seems my message would be much more emphatic if I dropped an F bomb right in middle of it.

I'm amazed at the words that jump into my mind during those intense times, and I am embarrassed to admit that I have to fight blurting them out. But that would jeopardize everything I stand for. I struggle with this every time I get fired up and don't want to slip, because I want to do everything I can to be consistent before my players and the One I serve. Because it would appear so out of character for me, I know the shock value alone would prove how serious I was, but it just wouldn't be worth it. John Wooden never used bad language, and he was the most successful coach in history.

I shudder to think what the kids who played for me on that first youth-league team would have thought if they had heard me swear or seen me throw tantrums. I still think about them today when my emotions run high. I'd hate to contradict all the things I said were so important.

The role faith played with the Warriors was no secret. Our logo was a shield bearing a cross. We didn't pick players on that basis, but we did look for coaches who were people of faith. I made it clear from the beginning that we wouldn't apologize for our Christian emphasis. We taught the kids about God and how important it was to live right—both why and how.

Besides that, I keep coming back to the question "Why am I here?" I owe it to my employers to do the absolute best job I know how. That's my priority every day. But I'd also like to think God has me in this position for a purpose, and I don't want to do anything to get in the way of that.

The press and the St. Louis fan base had a pretty good idea where I was coming from when I became manager, and I know a lot of them wondered if I had what it took to stand up and fight for my guys when necessary. That's a huge part of a manager's job. Sometimes a skipper even needs to get himself kicked out of a game, first to keep a player from getting booted, and second to prove to his guys how strongly he feels about a call and what it means to his team's fortunes.

Just a few games into my new role in 2012, I got tested. We were playing the Cubs in Chicago and were victimized by a bad call at the plate in a close game. The runner was clearly out, but he was called safe to tie the game, and our catcher, Yadi Molina, went nuts. I ran out there to argue the call and keep the attention off him—he's the last guy we want to lose, and I really got into it with the umpire.

Having been a catcher for so long, I know all the umpires by name, and despite all the grief I gave this one, he didn't toss me. In the ninth with the score tied, Yadi threw out a base-stealing specialist, and the second-base umpire called him safe. I shot out of that dugout like a cannon, this time determined not to come back until I was thrown out.

I stayed in that umpire's face until he finally had had enough and tossed me out of the game. I got into the visitors' clubhouse and my tiny office, slammed the door, and slouched in the chair behind my desk. As I feared, that Chicago runner soon scored the winning run.

The team came in as mad as I was. John Mabry, who was then our assistant hitting coach, peeked in and softly knocked. "Skip, you got a second?"

"Yeah, what's up?"

"You okay?"

I nodded.

"What'd you say to that ump?"

"I don't know. I was just yelling."

"Did you swear at him?"

"No."

"Then why did he throw you out?"

I said, "He told me he'd had enough, and I said, 'Well, I haven't.'"

"Let me get this straight," Mabry said. "You got thrown out of a major-league game for loitering?"

It was gratifying to be able to show that I didn't have to abandon my faith or my manhood to do my job. But even with instant replay, those men in blue and their questionable calls will put you to the test.

11

Respect the Ump— Even If He's Blind

KEY #5: CLASS

By now you know I don't claim to be an intellectual. I'm not a big word guy. But try this one on for size. *Dichotomy:* a contrast between two things that seem opposite of each other. That's what we're asking young athletes to be.

I'm a dichotomy because:

- I'm a jock with a college degree.
- For twenty-five years I wore catcher's equipment (the so-called "tools of ignorance"), but now, as a manager, I'm expected to know just what to do in every situation.
- I was raised to be a tough guy—a man's man—and to compete and take pride in winning. Yet as a Christian I'm to be—as Jesus Himself said—"wise as a serpent and gentle as a dove."

It has to make you shake your head and smile, doesn't it, that we're asking the kids we coach to grow up to become dichotomies, too? We're asking them to be a reckless warrior on the field and, at the same time, insisting they do all this with class. Tough assignment.

I ended the last chapter with a story of how I interacted with an umpire, which is the perfect place to launch this topic. It's one thing to get kids to treat their opponents with respect—shake their hands and say, "Good game," and mean it—win or lose. It's quite another to get them to extend that courtesy to umpires.

Being nasty to umpires has been a tradition for as long as most baseball fans can remember. Many fans feel it's just a fun part of the game, even their right, to berate them as boisterously as possible. At a big-league game you hear people scream all kinds of things at umps, and the more beer that's consumed, the louder they yell.

As far back as the famous "Casey at the Bat" poem, written by Ernest Thayer in 1888, someone in the stands shouts, "Kill him! Kill the umpire!" Later someone yells, "Fraud!"

These days people try to be funny, and the umpires have heard them all, including

- Did you get my Christmas card? It was in Braille!
- Should we turn off the lights so you can sleep?
- Is that Stevie Wonder behind the plate?
- You couldn't call hogs!
- We know you're blind; we've seen your wife!
- I saw your strike zone on a milk carton!
- Kick your dog, he's lying to you!
- Punch a hole in that mask!
- Is that your final answer?

As I mentioned in my letter to parents, it's simply a fact that at any level of amateur baseball you're going to run into spotty umpiring. Okay, at times bad umpiring. Okay, often really bad umpiring. If you're going to be a classy coach, parent, team, and player, you've got to learn to deal with this.

Resign yourself to the fact that by and large the umpiring at the lower levels is going to be bad, and set your team's expectations accordingly. Everybody expects inconsistency, but you need to prepare yourself and your players for the possibility that there will be days when their umpires are actually going to miss more calls than they get right. Just understand that this is part of the gig. Admittedly, it's hard to watch at times.

Every once in a great while you'll run into an angry ump with a chip on his shoulder who has something to prove or wants to show he's in charge. But usually bad umpiring is not intentional. In fact, it's just a result of inexperience, and the guy is doing his best to learn and get better. This is the perfect opportunity to teach your kids compassion and, yes, class. I know I use that word a lot, and by it I simply mean respectability. No doubt the word instantly brings to mind people you admire.

The person who responds to an ugly comment with a graceful one shows class.

The person who can calm another's anger with a soft answer exhibits class.

The person who passes up an opportunity to brag or preen or draw attention to himself, or who displays empathy by refusing to put someone else down, is classy.

If nothing else, you'll shock the life out of youth-league umpires if you treat them right. Because if you think the examples

I gave of coaches and parents overreacting to their kids' bad play were extreme, you should see how they treat umpires.

I asked my friend, major-league umpire and crew chief Ted Barrett, to give me his perspective. Here's a look from a man who has seen it at every level.

My wife and I raised three children in youth sports. We both helped coach, give rides, and provide snacks, so we know firsthand how much time, energy, and money goes into team sports. Still, that doesn't give anybody the right to lose their mind over every close play during the course of a season.

I know many thoughtful, intelligent, sensitive people who turn into complete morons when they feel an umpire has made a bad call. I've seen umpires abused verbally, seen things thrown at them, seen them followed to their cars, even heard people threaten their lives, all over a youth-baseball game!

Much of the problem is caused by the media focus on missed plays and unruly behavior by professional athletes. Yes, missed plays occur on rare occasions. What you don't see is what happens most nights: men playing by the rules and respecting officials.

Major-league players react to calls that don't go their way, but for the most part they respectfully don't cross the line. When they do they are often later ashamed of their actions and ask forgiveness, which is usually extended by the official. You don't hear the conversations players and umpires have later.

Here's something a player said to me a day after angrily arguing with me over a call. "Ted, I thought that guy was out, but when I saw the replay in slow-mo I could see he was safe. I don't know how you guys do it!"

Even when calls are missed, players usually understand. They know we have a tough job. Sure, they're upset at the time, but they get over it and move on.

Most youth baseball leagues can't find enough umpires to work their games. Would you want to do it? Most people think it looks easy until they try it. Many leagues use older teenagers, and those young men go out with little or no training and do their best to provide your child a safe, fair game, have a little fun, and earn a few dollars in the process. What does he get but idiots screaming at him and calling him names?

So much for the fun. He also gets an eleven- or twelve-year-old kid telling him he sucks, or worse, cussing him out (wonder where he got that?). You are so encouraging to your young players, yet you destroy this teenager as he tries to run a ball game? I fail to see the logic in that.

What are you so mad about? How about some support and understanding? And for you churchgoing people, how about giving an umpire a positive image as he sees you driving away with that sticker on the back of your car? Your negative behavior is more devastating to the cause of Christ than you know.

I know you want to win, but how about teaching our kids the importance of being honest? My friend Jerry Price writes about the time he took a new ball and made it dirty because the sun was going down and it would be tough to see. The umpire, his coach, and his dad got on him about cheating. Today he would be applauded for being crafty.

I've heard coaches teach their hitters to grab their hand

and pretend they got hit even when they didn't. Or if they chop the ball into the ground, they should limp like it hit their foot, trying to make the ump call it foul. Some call that gamesmanship. I call it what it is: cheating.

What are we teaching our kids?

Some say, "But if we don't do it, the other team will."

So let them cheat. Wouldn't you rather raise an honest child than one who cheats to get what he wants?

Go to the game and have fun. Don't yell at the umps working your kids' games, and don't come to a big-league game and yell at us. Just cheer on your team and enjoy the game.

Naturally, catchers have unique relationships with umpires, because we're almost touching the whole time we're working together, and in many cases we literally are. Some umps like to keep a hand on the catcher's back as a reference point.

Fans watching on TV can't know this, of course, and even those at big-league parks won't hear it, but catchers and umpires often have a running conversation throughout a game. I always enjoyed that. Catch long enough and build enough rapport and, before you know it, an ump will actually say things like, "Hey, Mike, where did you have that one?"

And I would say, "I got that one being a good pitch."

But I had to be honest with an ump like that, too, because if I was just trying to work him, he'd find out later. They're always being evaluated. If he started calling pitches I wanted him to call and then he saw on the video that he had broadened his strike zone too much, I'd lose all credibility with him.

But if I was honest with him and said, "That's a call we're going to have to have or this is going to be a six-hour game," he appreciated that.

And I appreciated it, too, when he would tell me when he missed a close call. To hear umpires say those sorts of things sure does change the whole flow of the game for a catcher.

We men behind the mask have a sort of fraternity, too, because we're in the most dangerous spot on the field. We look out for each other, just as human beings. When foul tips or errant pitches find those unprotected spots on our bodies, as they have a way of doing every game, or when a foul tip bangs off your mask so flush that it really rings your bell, there's an unwritten protocol.

When I would take a painful shot, the ump always knew, either from the way I grunted or flinched, or just from the way the ball sounded when it hit. You never want to show that something really hurts—I'll talk more about toughness later in the book—so you try to shake it off, but you appreciate every extra second you get for the sting or the ache to subside.

That's when the ump starts his charade. Without making a big scene, without even removing his mask, he'll ask if I'm all right. And unless I'm bleeding, can't breathe, have lost an appendage, or think I'm dying, I don't want the trainer or my manager to come out. So I assure him I am, but still he'll ask for the ball, take his time examining it, trade it out for another with the ball boy, and then decide he needs a whole new set for the bag at his waist.

Then, unless I've made it clear I'm eager to get things rolling again, he'll dust off the plate whether it needs it or not and take his time getting back into position. It's just common courtesy, no secret, and it happens all the time.

Catchers do the same for umpires. Sometimes the men in blue take an unimpeded foul tip directly into the chest protector, and you can just tell from the thud that it caught him pretty good. Or a foul tip will flip his mask around or catch him between the mask and his shoulder pad. Then we go through a similar routine. I ask if he's all right, ask for a new ball, and then, because I can't dust off the plate, I'll find a reason to go to the mound and chat with my pitcher.

I've been fortunate to work with some of the best umpires in the world. It's important to remember that even at the big-league level, these guys are people, too. Sometimes from the stands or sitting in front of the TV it looks like they're just nameless, faceless officials robotically going about their business. That's the way it should look, actually, and that's their goal. The ideal ump should be invisible. He shouldn't be the focal point, and he hopes every play is without controversy.

But because these are human beings with real lives, many with wives and families and homes and hopes and dreams and bills and physical problems, these guys are not immune to bad days, just like the rest of us. There's more continuing education and accountability than there has ever been, resulting in better umpires than at any other time in the history of the game. That said, it's helpful to know that even the best of the best have a tough time with such a difficult job.

ONE OF MY earliest memories of an umpire came during my rookie year in Milwaukee in 1994, when I was twenty-three. A crusty old veteran had the plate, and he made it very clear he was not happy about being at County Stadium on such a cold day and told me to tell my pitcher he had better not take any extra time out there.

I relayed the message, and the ump seemed to appreciate it, but the Texas Rangers were not as accommodating. A rookie hitter kept stepping out of the box and fixing his batting gloves, which drove the ump crazy. "Get back in there and be ready!" he barked, which just made the cocky kid take more time.

I felt a nudge in my back, forcing me farther outside than I wanted to go. I peeked back after the pitch and the ump nodded me farther outside. Now I was a few inches off the plate, and before the ball even hit my glove, I heard the loud strike three call. The kid only made things worse by giving the ump an earful before trudging back to the dugout.

The ump said, "Next time just have your pitcher hit your glove. I don't care if you're two feet off the plate."

Of course, that's not my idea of class or sportsmanship, and it shows that umpires make mistakes, too, just like players. Nobody wants to strike out four times and commit a handful of errors. You feel like you're on an island and nobody can save you. What does a bad game look like for an umpire? The first time I saw one changed forever how I view the men in blue.

It happened to an ump who had been around a few years and had never gone out of his way to attract attention. He always did a pretty good job calling balls and strikes, but this day was different. We were in St. Louis in the first inning when he tapped me on the shoulder and said, "Hey, Mike, I'm not picking up the ball very well today."

How was that possible? I was thinking, *You've got one job!* But the longer the inning wore on, the more obvious it became that he wasn't joking. He hesitated, his timing was off, and his calls didn't ring with authority, so you could tell he was doubting himself. And every call seemed to rouse one dugout or the other.

First I was mad. Then it hit me: I've been there myself, many times. Some days the most routine play seems like an impossible task; then you start fighting yourself, which only makes everything worse. This poor guy started calling strikes balls and balls strikes, and I mean pitches that weren't even close. I flew past frustrated and just felt sorry for him. I tried to calm my pitcher and even talked to the coaches between innings.

It turned out to be a long day for all of us, especially the guy behind me. He got both barrels from anybody within earshot, but through it all, I learned an important lesson. Even at the major-league level, these guys are human. They're going to make mistakes, and some days, just like the rest of us, they're going to just stink—yes, even the best in the world.

My point? How can we expect a fifteen-year-old who's been given a four-day crash course to get every call right when the best in the game can't even do that? You know youth-league umpires are doing their best, but while they're feeling the pressure to please everybody, remember everything they've been taught, and control the game, parents and coaches are coming unglued and players are treating them like scum.

That's why we insisted that our boys not even shrug or sigh or frown in the face of a bad call. And if an umpire cost them a game, or even a whole tournament, every player on our team was to shake the umpire's hand, just as they would their opponents'.

That's not easy, but that's what a classy team does.

And then you know what I had to do? I had to admit to my players that I had made mistakes in that game, too. Devastating as it was to lose that way, it presented a great opportunity to point out that our mistakes led up to that call that cost us the win. Yes, the ump missed the call, but I also made a mistake that inning by sending a runner who was thrown out at the plate. We win together, we lose together, and we refuse to point fingers at one another or the umpires.

I had to remind myself of this mantra the first time I coached one of my own sons, and our twelve-and-under team was fortunate enough to reach the championship game of a local tournament. The boys had competed well, and we looked forward to their tasting a little well-earned success.

Calling balls and strikes behind the plate was a boy not much older than the players, and much as he tried to appear ready for the job, he really shouldn't have been put in that position for a tournament final.

It turned out to be a sloppy game full of errors by both teams and several missed calls by the umpires. We coaches and the parents and our players handled it all very well, and after the lead changed hands several times, we fought back to tie the game in the top of the last inning. If we could just hold them in the bottom half and get into extra innings, the top of our lineup was due up.

After a hit and a couple of misplays, they had a man on third with two out. Just as our pitcher came set, the plate umpire yelled, "Balk!" loud and proud. I had been watching closely, and as a career catcher, I know the balk rules. He hadn't so much as flinched or done anything that would have deceived the runner.

As the runner was awarded home, the other team and their fans erupted, and rightfully so. Our guys were dumbfounded and didn't even know how to react. I went out and quickly tried to get an explanation for the call. The ump told me he had seen the pitcher turn the ball in his hand as he brought his arms up, and he interpreted that as deceiving.

I tried to prevail upon the other umpire to agree that the move was completely natural and had been done dozens of times throughout the game by pitchers on both sides. But the plate ump assured me he had just studied the rule book, and this was a judgment call that could not be overturned.

The kid was trying to be the best umpire he could be. He was just going about it the wrong way. He had been conscientious by studying to sharpen his skills, but he hadn't had anyone help him decipher the rules. You see it often, and it's unfortunate, but inexperienced umps and referees tend to do this a lot. They find an interesting, obscure rule and convince themselves someone has violated it in the very next game they officiate.

Still, I was proud of our boys. After I thanked the ump for his explanation, I shook both umpires' hands, and when my team finished congratulating the winners, they shook the umpires' hands, too. Because that's what we always do, win or lose.

INCONSISTENT OFFICIATING HAPPENS everywhere in every sport, and it's not likely to change anytime soon. One of the best things an organization can do is to make it mandatory for all coaches, and as many parents as possible, to umpire a youth game, to see just how difficult it can be. We would all learn to be more tolerant.

Regardless of whether you get that opportunity, imagine yourself in another person's shoes—your boss, your spouse, your coworker—before you confront or criticize them. You may find that's an accurate measure of your level of class—and character.

12

Stay in Your Lane

KEY #6: CHARACTER

Always go to other people's funerals, otherwise they won't come to yours.
—YOGI BERRA

Young people show signs of maturity when they begin to consider what they would like to be remembered for. While that may sound like something that should be put off until the twilight of one's life, you need to give this some thought when you're young enough to do something about it.

I'm not talking about self-fulfillment, like becoming rich and famous, but rather inward pursuits—like becoming a loyal friend, a good parent, or someone others describe as

- Loyal
- Trustworthy
- Generous
- Eager to pass wisdom on to the next generation
- Positive

- Humble
- Selfless

Those are things we should all want to be remembered for; they serve as the very definitions of character. As Abraham Lincoln said, "Reputation is the shadow. Character is the tree."

ONE OF MY favorite examples of consistency and character as a player was Jim Thome, who retired in 2012 and now works in the White Sox front office. Jim played twenty-two seasons for six different teams and finished seventh all-time in home runs with 612. He was a five-time all-star and may be one of the most respected players ever.

The first time you meet Big Jim you wonder if it's possible for any big leaguer, let alone one that accomplished, to be that nice and genuine. But if you think it's an act, you're wrong. Jim was a fierce competitor but also a model of how to treat people with respect.

I'll never forget calling Jim once during the middle of a season when his team was caught up in a lot of drama—fights in the clubhouse, controversy in the media, and debates over everything but baseball. I asked him how he seemed to stay above it all, despite his leadership role on the team.

He said, "Mike, I just stay in my lane."

How simple, yet wise and profound. I know Jim was doing everything he could to help his team sort through the adversity, but when it came to all the emotion, he didn't allow himself to drift into that lane.

This is a trap many parents of young athletes fall into. Inevitably, coaches are going to make decisions you won't be happy about, just like many of my decisions don't make Cardinals fans happy. The difference is, Cardinals fans pay a lot of money for the right to scream at me or call their favorite sports talk show and say how they would run the ball club. I cheerfully accept their right to weigh in as part of one of the best jobs in the world. I can take it and continue trying to do the best I can to keep us playing as deep into October as possible.

But when youth-league parents swerve into the gossip lane, rationalizing that they're just "discussing" the coach "for the good of the team," it's a whole different story. That coach doesn't have the resources a big-league manager has. He doesn't have the best players on the planet at his beck and call, or the finest equipment and training facilities and stadium and grounds crew and support staff available. He's not even getting paid.

The fact is, maybe you're right and he's wrong. Maybe he doesn't know the game as well as you do. He's a volunteer. Help him out. Talk to him face-to-face. Be part of the solution, not the problem. The reality is that a lack of character in the stands tears teams apart and confuses the kids.

Parents are always going to be emotionally involved when it comes to their kids, and rightfully so. But if you're looking for the best possible experience for your son or daughter, take the advice of future Hall of Famer Jim Thome and stay in your lane—supporting your child by also supporting the coach and the decisions he or she makes.

On our youth team, we made a conscious effort to make a bigger deal of the character stuff than the baseball stuff. We always made it a point to notice and recognize a boy who would do a task none of the others wanted to. Or when one showed sportsmanship to an opponent. For instance, the boy who would go out of his way to encourage a disappointed teammate was celebrated, and then it became contagious.

Amazing how the things we adults deem important soon become the same for those we lead.

TRUTH BE TOLD, it wasn't always easy setting the example I wanted the kids to follow. Sometimes I was tested in the trenches, like when opposing-team players had what seemed like zero supervision and were allowed to huff and slam their thighs with their gloves when they didn't like the umpire's call. Or when they yelled at our hitters during each pitch or called our kids' names. You can imagine what I would have liked to do.

My team was watching me, and I had to bite my tongue. Many responses came to mind, but these were always great opportunities to teach. The kids knew what I was thinking, because they were thinking the same thing. I needed to make them understand that stooping to the other team's level wasn't going to happen: we weren't going to retaliate. We were going to maintain our dignity. Even if this obnoxious team beat us, we would shake their hands and tell them, "Good game."

If we beat them and they chose to slap our hands or ignore our hands, that would be on them, not us. We would be the bigger men and offer to shake everybody's hand, including the umpires'.

There would never, ever be any yelling from our bench except to encourage our own teammates during the game, and that was something I demanded. We needed to show some life, like we enjoyed being there and pulling for our guys.

Our parents would often tell me how badly they wanted to defend their kids and give it back to the other team as good as we were getting it. But not responding in kind was one of our nonnegotiables. We would not fall into the trap of barking at the other team.

You want to know how hard that can be? Let me tell you about the time I came the closest to taking somebody's head off.

During a tournament over Father's Day weekend, our first baseman came back to the dugout after I noticed he'd had a conversation with the adult first-base coach from the other team. It was obvious he was bothered and didn't want to tell me what had gone on, but I insisted.

He reluctantly told me the coach was swearing at him for slapping hard tags on his kids on pickoff attempts. The next half inning I switched with my assistant coach and coached first base instead of third so I could be close to the other team's bench. I didn't want to make a big scene, but I casually asked to talk to the head coach and the first-base coach and calmly asked for his side of the story.

He looked and sounded guilty while insisting our kid was tagging too hard. I said, "If you've got a problem with that, you talk to me and I'll deal with it. And maybe you use language like that with your players, but I am not going to let you do it with mine."

As fate would have it, we faced the same team the next day in the championship game. When my first baseman stepped into the box, the first pitch sailed up and in and hit him in the back. I made sure he was okay, and as he trotted to first base I slowly walked back toward the coaching box at third, praying about how to handle this without exploding.

I stopped in front of the opposing dugout and made eye contact with the coaches. The one who apparently enjoyed bullying kids had a look like he couldn't wait for me to do something that would make for great conversation at the bar after his next slow-pitch softball game. If I had done what I wanted, he wouldn't have played again until the following summer. If anybody ever deserved a lesson . . .

But everything I had taught these boys, everything our organization stood for would have been trashed in a few seconds of revenge. Thank God, I had enough sense to just shake my head and say, "Really?"

Part of me felt like I had let my little Warrior down by not doing what I had been trained for years to do when things like this popped up during a big-league game. But this wasn't the big leagues. This was youth-league baseball. This was the time to exhibit some character, to be the bigger man.

Now, before you slam this book shut and label me just another turn-the-other-cheek Bible-thumper, hear me out. I don't apologize for being a Bible guy. But I also believe strongly in standing up for those entrusted to my care and fighting for what is right. I believe too many men fail to fight for the things we should fight for, like our families, our marriages, and our faith.

The message to coaches is this: When the boys become adults, they will learn quickly when retaliation is appropriate to protect their teammates. This is not something to try to teach or master at the youth level, especially in the heat of battle with tempers flaring.

When an adult threatens a kid or assigns one of his to harm another, he needs to have his head examined. Adults need to step up and call out an idiot when they see one and do everything in their power to ensure that person is never again given the honor of being called coach.

THIS KIND OF bad behavior reminds me of a phrase everybody has heard: "It's not where you start, it's where you finish."

I believe that the time to start thinking about your legacy is not at the end but at the beginning, because as I said, that's when you're able to do something about it. That's the reason we coaches spent so much time emphasizing character building with the first version of our youth baseball team, when we were known as the Wolverines.

Over those first years, we developed a board of advisers that any Fortune 500 company would be proud of. Movers and shakers in the St. Louis community—presidents of banks, construction companies, tech firms, and other large companies, some of whom had sons on the team and others who just believed in our mission—volunteered to help us.

Then I decided to rename the organization, at that time three teams (now seven), the Missouri Warriors, a name with deeper meaning. Our long-term goal for these young athletes was to help them develop into warriors for their families, their faith, and their community. We were willing to pull the plug if it didn't work, but we fully believed this would be a twenty-year investment, and we were committed not only to helping these kids reach their athletic dreams but to serving as mentors and resources as they tackled the challenges of education and life in general.

The organization had been getting recognized locally, and frankly, I liked the fact that not much of that had a lot to do with wins and losses. The experiment was working, and the parents were championing the concept. Many of the same ones who thought my letter was pretty crazy had witnessed firsthand the freedom the kids had to just play the game—and also the freedom they themselves enjoyed to just be parents and not have to bear their sons' athletic futures on their shoulders. They simply came and watched and let the coaches do the coaching.

It was the most enjoyable youth-sports experience I had ever been around, and most of the other parents felt the same. It seemed everywhere we played we were approached by tournament directors, umpires, opposing coaches, and parents, commenting on the hustle and discipline of the boys, but mostly on the way our parents and coaches conducted themselves.

Every practice and game ended with an individual talk with each boy (without parent involvement) in which he was given a list of homework items to improve on before the next practice or game. It became obvious who took this seriously and who didn't, and that determined whom we kept on the team.

That resulted in difficult conversations with friends whose boys weren't willing to work at getting better. Some great kids wanted only to have fun, and we had to walk that line between keeping it fun but also following the first of my three main goals (to teach these boys how to play baseball the right way).

To be sure we stayed in our own lane, we had a responsibility to the kids who wanted to get better and compete in an atmosphere of excellence. So, we further defined the culture we were trying to create. It still wasn't about attracting only the best talent we could find, but neither could we move forward with kids who didn't want to work to get better. This was all about attitude.

These boys needed to know that we could have fun but that the greatest rewards in life, truly having fun, involved hard work and self-sacrifice. We didn't let players go because of their talent level or lack thereof. If a boy was committed to the team and to getting better and bought into the idea of growing as a young man, we wanted him to stay with us, regardless of his talent level.

That proved a tricky line to walk after all the preaching I had done about just letting the kids enjoy the game. I had to concede that if their idea of enjoying the game meant just playing *at* it and not committing themselves to playing it the right way, then our program wasn't the right fit and perhaps they should just join a casual park team that played and didn't really train.

As I mentioned before, I also had to let kids go whose parents couldn't abide by the rule that we coaches would not allow them to lobby for their kids to have more playing time or a certain spot in the batting order. That was no fun, but I knew if we allowed it, we would end up like every other program, and that didn't interest me at all. There may have been those who wished we would waver on the clarity of our mission, but that wasn't even a temptation.

By the end of the summer, we were not only holding our own, but we were winning, and the parents who had stuck with us were having so much fun that they wanted the team to play into the fall. The coaches and I decided we were at a good stopping point to keep the kids hungry for the game. It worked well, as they all showed up the next year, eager to continue getting better.

I'M A BIG believer in the idea that we learn more from hardship and failure than we do from success, which is a key aspect in developing character as well. This ties in with the philosophy of establishing your legacy when you're young, too. While I had a big dream—I mean, there's not much more unrealistic a dream a kid can have than becoming a big leaguer—I never had an inflated view of my abilities, and nothing was ever handed to me. I think if it had been, I'd never have made it.

When I reflect on my life and career, it's a series of highs and lows where it seems I had to fight and scratch and claw to get anywhere, and then do the same to stay there. I'm not denying

I was blessed with some natural ability and was a gifted athlete from a fairly young age. And, despite the list of valleys I'm about to describe, I don't want to sound like a complainer either. I wouldn't trade my life, or my journey, for anything. I'm grateful for every obstacle, because everything I've been through has shaped me in some way.

Sometimes kids don't want to hear about the tough times in a big-league career. To them a life in baseball sounds glamorous. Make no mistake, there's nothing like it. Anyone who has ever tasted it only leaves it kicking and screaming and longing for one more season, one more series, one more game. I sure did.

But it's a tough grind, too, and unless you're one of the elite, shoo-in Hall of Famers, baseball can be a cruel game at times. You're never sure you've secured your starting spot. You always wonder if you can be honest about how bad your injury is (everybody, and I mean everybody, plays hurt). You're always a slump away from being sent back to the minors, and there's never a guarantee you'll be back.

My career was exceptional in only three ways: its longevity (especially for a catcher); that I got to play in the postseason four times, including a World Series; and because of my defense. I won four Gold Gloves in five years, led the National League twice in runners caught stealing, and was among the top three in the league for five straight years in fielding percentage, twice finishing first. I set a major-league record for catchers by playing in 252 straight games without an error. During that time I set another record by fielding 1,565 consecutive chances without an error.

Not too many people know that, because those aren't the kinds of statistics baseball fans care about and memorize. They won't get a player into the Hall of Fame. And I've never mentioned them when coaching or counseling or mentoring a young ballplayer. While it's important to celebrate your peaks, I'm more likely to talk about character, and as I've said, character is forged not on the mountaintop but in the valley.

I PLAYED IN fewer than thirty games for the Brewers my rookie year before they sent me down to the New Orleans AAA ball club to see if I could improve on my hitting. I didn't do much better there and was asked to play winter ball in the Dominican Republic during the off-season. There I would get big-league competition and more playing time.

In 1995, I was back up with the big-league team and hitting a little better, but I was the backup catcher and getting very little playing time. At the end of the season, general manager Sal Bando called me into his office at County Stadium and asked if I'd be interested in playing in Puerto Rico during the winter. I had been looking forward to some downtime to spend with Kristin and our two little ones, Tate and Katie, but my agent at the time told me he thought I had a good shot at taking over the starting job in Milwaukee if I had a good off-season.

Luckily for me, Kristin agreed to bring the kids and come along. We rented a condo on the beach and felt like we were on vacation every day, up until the time I had to leave for the ball field. I played fairly well and actually was named to the all-star team ahead of Iván "Pudge" Rodríguez, who, in all fairness, wasn't playing every day. (He would go on to be one of the best catchers in the history of the game.)

Our team was the unlikely winner of the league, and at the end of the championship parade and celebration, the town awarded me the key to the city. (I'd had a pretty good winter, but not that good, so I was blown away by their generosity. Not many American players stayed the entire time, and the team had not won a championship in many years.) I later found out there was a young, aspiring catcher in the stands watching the parade and the presentation: Yadier Molina.

That spring of 1996, the Brewers made no moves to sign any free-agent catchers and informed me they believed I was ready to take the reins. Everything was going well during spring training in Chandler, Arizona, until there were about six games to go before opening day. Then an overzealous kid from the Angels, trying to make a name for himself, bowled me over at the plate and I felt something pop in my knee.

I ignored it and finished the game, and back in my room that night I flexed it and iced and heated and iced it again. In the morning, I could barely stand. I was in trouble.

Before dawn I somehow made my way over to the stadium and hobbled into the cage to see if I could even get into the catching position. I could, but there would be no fooling anyone this time. I slipped into the trainers' room and could tell by the looks on their faces that it was as serious as I feared. They made me go talk to Manager Phil Garner.

I was nearly in tears, twenty-five years old and about to become a big-league starter for the first time, and Gar insisted I go immediately for an MRI. Now that I'm a manager, I know exactly what he did as soon as I left his office: he got on the phone with Sal, looking for another starting catcher. That's no easy task with less than a week left in spring training.

The MRI showed a tear in both my meniscus and my posterior cruciate ligament. The doctor told me I should probably have arthroscopic surgery, which would take me out for several weeks, but he added, "You could play with it and have the operation done after the season, if you can handle the pain."

That was all I needed to hear. I ran with a terrible hobble all year, but I was catching really well. As usual, I didn't hit much, but I caught almost every day, around 100 of the first 110 or so games.

Finally, contributing almost nothing offensively, I was called into Garner's office. "I hate to do this, Mike," he said, "because you've been so great defensively and everybody can see that, but we have to send you down."

I was devastated, but caught twenty games for the AAA club in New Orleans before being called back up to the Brewers in September. I played here and there in another half dozen games as the season was winding down. Then, at about three in the morning on September 27 in Detroit, with three days to go until the end of the season, Kristin woke me up with a phone call. She had gone into labor with our third child almost two weeks early and was on her way to the hospital in St. Louis.

I've teased her since that she should've known better than to do that during the season. She had our first two kids Cesarean, and so of course we assumed this one would be the same.

Gar didn't even sound annoyed that my call woke him during the wee hours. He agreed I needed to catch the next flight home. As soon as I landed I called St. Luke's Hospital to find out whether she'd had a boy or a girl, and I was stunned to find out she had told the doctor to cancel the C-section and let the birth progress naturally in the hope that I would make it in time.

I rushed over there, and no more than thirty minutes after I arrived, so did Luke.

It had been some year. Kristin and I had really been on an emotional roller coaster. I enjoyed sharing the great news with the Brewers, but I wasn't expecting the call I got the next day from Phil. He asked if I would be interested in flying back to Detroit for the last game of the year. He promised he'd start me if I did.

I always had the utmost respect for Gar, and he had treated me great. He believed in me and saw in me the catcher I would one day become. I owed him a lot and would've done almost anything for him. Almost.

After grinding through the whole season with the bad knee and never once asking for a day of rest, then getting sent down to AAA after catching a hundred big-league games and doing a pretty darn good job defensively, I was frustrated and physically and emotionally beat. Dragging your family back and forth from Milwaukee to New Orleans after a winter in Puerto Rico is just part of the life of a young ballplayer, but I had had enough.

After all of this, I know where I'm supposed to be.

"Can you be here for the game tomorrow?"

"No, Skip, you know what? I need to stay here."

It was out of character for me to say no to the organization and especially to Gar, and I figured my decision would hurt my chances for the following year, but I could tell Kristin was glad I did.

During the off-season I went to a knee surgeon to get the work done. When he saw the damage, he said, "You caught how many games on this knee?"

I told him 106 in the majors and 20 in triple-A.

"That's a miracle."

As it turned out, this was another lesson learned in the valley that proves instructive for youth-league ballplayers. I was the Milwaukee Brewers' starting catcher almost every day for the next two seasons.

BECOMING A FULL-TIME big-league starter is only a dream until you become one, and while there's nothing like it, reality also sets in hard and fast. It may feel glamorous at the beginning, and players may face temptations that make it hard to stay in their lanes. Also, a six-month regular season is a marathon, especially for a catcher. I don't know anyone who regrets landing such a job, but any sense of accomplishment that comes with it is hard earned by digging deep for reserves of toughness you sometimes wonder whether you have within.

And much like whatever in your life puts you to the test, that grind showed me what I was made of.

13

Nothing Worth Doing Right Is Easy

KEY #7: TOUGHNESS

I would love to have learned a few things the easy way. I can't say I ever grew fond of the valleys of life, but I sure know the territory. As I say, a lesson learned there is a lesson learned forever. Again, I'm not complaining. I'm into my third decade with a wife who's as beautiful on the inside as she is on the outside and who still carries way more than her share of the load because of the toll baseball exacts on our family. We've got five great kids, wonderful friends, and I enjoy a challenging, fulfilling job I never dreamed I'd have—and now can't imagine doing anything else.

But getting here? Oh, boy.

You'd think after that Year of the Knee in '96 and then catching 231 games over the next two seasons for the Brewers, I would have settled into a nice career as a starting catcher. I had heard—and parroted—all my life, "Nothing worth doing right is easy." I guess I had to live that out just so my counsel to the next generation would carry the ring of truth.

In late May of 1998 I was twenty-seven and in my third full season as Milwaukee's starting catcher. The Brewers had been moved from the American League to the National at the beginning of the season, and we were struggling, below .500, as were the visiting Pirates that Tuesday night the twenty-sixth.

It was nice to have Kristin in town, and she had a great seat, just a couple of rows from the field. As usual, I had been having a tough time at the plate, swinging at so many low breaking balls that my skipper, Phil Garner, made me give him a new sleeve of golf balls every time I struck out on one. I told a reporter last year that I gave Gar so many, he's probably still using some of them.

Most good defensive catchers aren't expected to hit much, but I never resigned myself to that. I played to my strengths, but I constantly labored to shore up my weaknesses, too. I never did become a great hitter, but for as long as I played, I worked at it.

I was busting my tail to stay in there that night and really see the ball, and in the bottom of the seventh, my RBI single tied the game at 1. The Pirates scored again in the eighth, but I got another chance in the bottom of the ninth with two on and one out. It wasn't going to be easy, as I had to face 6'5", 225-pound right-hander Rich Loiselle, who could really bring it.

His 0-1 fastball sailed up and in on me, and I barely had time to flinch before it drilled me flush on the left cheek with such a loud pop it could be heard on television and several rows into the seats. How I didn't go down, I'll never know. I've often been asked, and I just don't have a good answer. Any closer to my eye and that would have been a sure career ender and might have even been life-threatening.

So many things ran through my mind at once. First, I wanted to get to first to load the bases—though there was no way I was staying in the game with my mouth filling with blood so fast I was about to choke, plus both the Pirates catcher and the umpire were already frantically waving for help.

Then I was mad, though I knew it hadn't been intentional. The last thing Loiselle wanted was another base runner in that situation, and I certainly wasn't a dangerous enough hitter to brush back. But I always hated when pitchers threw close enough to any batter's head, let alone mine.

I knew Kristin saw and heard what had happened. I stood in the box with one hand on my hip and the other holding my bat; then I reached for my cheek, feeling for whether the ball had broken the skin. It hadn't, but now I had to spit, and I produced such a mouthful of blood that people gasped.

Not even ten seconds after I'd been hit, Gar and our trainer were out there, and even the umpire had a hand on my back. I was rushed to the emergency room, where I needed stitches. Most important to me was learning that the next hitter, our shortstop José Valentín, had won the game with a single to center.

I had lost some teeth (eventually most of them on that side of my mouth), and I came back with a purple face swollen to nearly twice its normal size. I found my teammate Jeff Cirillo and asked him if it was true that I hadn't gone down, as the details had begun to grow fuzzy. I was glad to hear that I hadn't.

When I got to Gar's office, he sat there grinning at my grotesque face while he puffed on his ever-present stogie. I said, "If you've ever done me a favor, Skip, I want to be in the lineup tomorrow."

He shook his head. "You serious?"

"I am."

"Can you even get the mask on?"

"I'll make it work."

"It's your call, Mike."

I think he was impressed and wanted to make a statement to the rest of the team. As a manager now, I love it when I have a player who gets hurt but still wants to be in there and produce. To be clear, it's a different story when you're dealing with a youngster and it's your—and his parents'—responsibility to look out for his long-term well-being. At that level, winning isn't the end-all goal, and a kid should sit out till he's healthy.

With the Brewers in '98, stitches and all, I believed I could help us win.

I didn't tell Gar that even running killed me and that our trainer would have to change my bandages between innings. I heard that our backup catcher, Bobby Hughes, said, "You mean I don't get to start even when he gets hit in the face?"

Before the umpires went out to their spots at the start of the game, they asked me to take off my mask so they could see my face.

I went hitless in ten innings, but I did throw out a runner, and we won 3-2. Playing may have been one of my dumber decisions, but I admit I got a kick out of one of the fans spray painting a sheet that read: "Matheny—The Toughest Man in Baseball."

Obviously I'd rather not have endured that—and put Kristin through it—just to pick up a cool nickname and have a tale to tell. But it doesn't take a genius to see the transferable principle, especially for young athletes. If I could have avoided taking that fastball to the face, I would have, but the point was, it was the ninth inning, and I was trying to stay in there and fight. That's what I urge coaches to teach today—from beginners to big leaguers. I don't care if you're a weak-hitting defensive specialist or leading the majors in RBIs. You're up there to grind out every at bat.

It has gotten back to me that some of my current Cardinals have seen that grainy video from the previous century, and they're impressed that the young version of their skipper took one in the chops for his team and didn't go down. One praised me to a reporter: "What an animal." I have to admit it made me smile. I'll take that.

Another told a sportswriter, "That says something about what kind of guy he is, the type of competitor. I've seen some of the hits he's taken as a catcher." Interesting he should say that, because in truth it was those hits that would define me as a player. Not to mention end my career.

By the end of the 1998 season, I had been a professional for seven years, in the big leagues with the Brewers for five, and had caught 445 games. I had been paid nearly four times as much for my last season as for the previous one and was now eligible for salary arbitration. That can be an exciting time for a starter, unless your career batting average is .231 and your ball club thinks it can find someone better.

In December I was granted free agency. That's a rough, scary time, knowing you're in the prime of your physical life but having no idea whether any big-league team finds that good enough to want you on their roster. Fortunately, two days later, the team that had first drafted me out of high school ten years before, the Toronto Blue Jays, signed me for the 1999 season. I caught fifty-seven games as Darrin Fletcher's backup and was again released after the season, facing the same uncertainty as the year before.

How's that for the glamour of big-league baseball?

My big break came when I signed with St. Louis on

December 15, 1999, and I began the best five-year stretch of my career. That's where I became a starter again, won a few Gold Gloves, played in those postseasons and that World Series, set those errorless games records, and got to play for Tony La Russa.

But as I say, all those hits I took had already been taking their toll—probably for a lot longer than anyone, including me, had any idea. The sad fact is that catchers have always considered standing their ground and taking hits as badges of honor, signs of manhood. I know I did.

I felt honored and appreciated when Tony, one of the most highly respected managers in the game, pleaded with me to stop planting myself in front of the plate when a runner was bearing down on me. He'd tell me there was nothing wrong with avoiding the violent collision and sweep-tagging the runner.

Really, down deep I wanted to be valuable to Tony, so indispensable that he didn't want to lose me. So how did I thank him? Did I say, "Well, thanks so much, Skip, I'll do exactly that, and I appreciate your looking out for me"?

Not on your life. I got mad. I would actually say to the future Hall of Famer, "Sure, and you want me to wear a skirt out there, too?" Needless to say, he didn't like that much.

That might not have been the best choice of words for the husband of a D-1 field hockey player and now the father of one of the toughest lady ice hockey players at Ohio State. But back then, you couldn't have paid me enough to step out of the way of a runner and sweep-tag him. What kind of a self-respecting catcher could do that and then look at himself in the mirror the next morning and call himself a man?

Talk about lessons learned the hard way, learning to know when you're wrong, being willing to apologize, no strings attached. . . .

Guilty, guilty, guilty.

Do as I say, not as I did. I now manage the most valuable catcher in the game—maybe in history. Had Major League Baseball not changed the rule concerning collisions at home plate, requiring runners to slide and catchers to apply sweep tags—with me as vocal as anyone leading the way for the change—I would be pleading with Yadier Molina to do what Tony tried to get me to do.

Because Yadi's so good that I don't want to lose him?

Sure, but not only that. You'd think a career catcher would be sympathetic to a man not wanting to appear weak, wanting to defend the dish, put his body on the line for the win.

I have personal experience. When did I switch sides?

When reality came knocking, literally. One too many times.

No one knows how many concussions a person can endure before the damage is done. One? A half dozen? More? The research is still in its infancy. Look at the mess the NFL is in. Was it one good shot I took that pushed me over the edge? Was it several over a short period? Who can say?

I can't even tell you when I suffered my first concussion. I was guarding the plate like the big leaguers did when I was a kid, bracing myself for impact. Can a seventy- or eighty-pound child hitting another one the same size at full speed give him a concussion?

Such injuries usually happen when the catcher is knocked down and the back of his head slams against the ground. Rarely is he knocked unconscious. I never was. In high school football, usually on defense, we led with our heads, and I recall telling my teammates, "That didn't feel right."

They would respond, "Yeah, but didn't it feel great?"

And I'd say, "Yeah! 'Course it felt great!" And it did! It made me feel like Superman.

Sometimes you'd get your bell rung, what we called it when you'd see double for a second or your hearing would go in and out or you'd feel dazed, and then some coach would give you the stupid test: "How many fingers am I holding up?" or "What day is it?" or "Do you know where you are?"

Now we know that a kid ought to be immediately taken out of a game, checked over, maybe not practice for a week, maybe even have a brain scan. But for years, if he could tell you it was Saturday and you were holding up two fingers and he felt fine, he went right back into the game.

We catchers learned to grab our helmet and our mask, slap it back on our heads, and assure everybody we were okay. You didn't come out of a game unless you were bleeding or a bone was showing. That's what being a catcher was all about.

How many concussions must I have suffered before I even got to Michigan? How many there? How many in the minors? By the time I got to St. Louis for those glory days under Tony, when I came into my own as a Gold Glover, I had caught over 500 games and would catch more than 600 more for the Cardinals.

More than 180 games in San Francisco gave me over 1,300 in the majors, on top of more than 360 in the minors. I couldn't begin to guess how many collisions I had endured at the plate or how many times I took the worst of it. It never mattered. What mattered was making the play, never backing down, taking the punishment, doing what I had to do for the win, for the team. My reputation? I wasn't a rah-rah guy. I was known as the guy who kept his mouth shut and did his job. And I've got to tell you, honestly, I was proud of that reputation. I wanted to be the one everybody could count on.

If I was pressed, I could maybe dredge up a couple dozen or more times in my professional career when I was really nailed at the plate. I never felt they were intentional, though once I followed a guy into his dugout after tagging him for the third out. Both benches emptied because they thought I was going after him due to how hard he had hit me, but the truth was, I didn't know where I was at first.

But I never once left a game. How many times should I have? Looking back, plenty. But we just didn't do that.

I began my thirteenth big-league season in the spring of 2006 at age thirty-five. One game in late May I took a typical foul tip in the mask, which is right where you want to take them. Despite all the protective equipment you see on a catcher, there are all kinds of exposed spots the ball can find, and it does, all the time. If you've ever seen a catcher in the clubhouse with his uniform off, you've seen a man with bruises up and down his arms, around his collarbone and neck above where his chest protector sits, on his thighs, and of course on his throwing hand, much as he tries to hide it.

A foul tip into the chest protector isn't too bad, but if it's a direct shot, it can be worse than it looks. So taking one into the mask is what you prefer. The mask is padded all the way around, and sometimes a glancing blow will twist it off your face, but it's extremely rare for a ball to hurt you if it hits the mask. It feels like someone has punched you in the forehead, but without the pain.

Well, I took one the hitter barely tipped, and it skipped cleanly over my glove straight into the wire mesh. Because I'd taken thousands of those over the years, I didn't give it much thought. A few pitches later I took an identical one. Then another. No big deal.

Except that suddenly I was having trouble picking up the ball as it left the pitcher's hand. I blinked and squinted and wondered if those foul tips had hit harder than I thought.

My vision still wasn't sharp when we got the third out and I trotted into the dugout, so I sat next to Stan Conte (who was in his fifteenth year as the Giants' trainer and is now vice president of medical services for the Dodgers). I said casually, "Have you ever heard of anybody having trouble with foul balls?"

Fortunately, he was a pretty aggressive trainer. He shot me a double take and said, "Wait a second, Mike. What're you talking about?"

I shrugged. "I just noticed I had a little trouble focusing after that last foul tip."

He said he'd keep an eye on me.

The next night I took another one in the same spot. The same thing happened with my eyesight, and when I peeked into the dugout Stan was staring at me. When I came in he asked me to tell him what was happening. All I could tell him was that I could see the ball but not the way I liked and needed to see it.

The last few days of May we flew to Miami to play the Marlins, and Stan was watching very closely, to the point where I regretted I had said anything. He'd been researching the issue, but I didn't want to hear about it. I just wanted to see more clearly. I caught one of our hard throwers in an early game and took another tip off the mask, and I didn't even want to look at Stan.

I took a lot of pride in not being a soft guy. But I was starting to get spooked, because I realized something was wrong.

On May 31, 2006, I was catching Matt Morris against the Marlins. He and I had been teammates in St. Louis, and I liked working with him. We thought alike, and he was one fierce competitor.

Nobody but Stan and I knew what was going on, but I took two consecutive tips to the mask, and when I came in after that inning, I could barely keep my eyes open. I couldn't believe I wanted to fall asleep in the middle of a major-league baseball game. Stan came over and sat next to me, but I wouldn't even talk to him. I was scared and I was mad.

When I went back out, I noticed that more than my vision and my energy level were a problem. I wasn't thinking clearly. I tried to pull myself together, but my mind wasn't working.

The Marlins got a runner to second, and as I was going through my signs to Matt, I was afraid the runner was going to tip off the pitch to the hitter. So I asked for time and jogged to the mound, told Matt what to throw, and told him to ignore whatever sign I flashed.

By the time I got back behind the plate, I had forgotten what I had told him, so I emphatically signaled a curveball, he nodded, and threw the fastball I had originally told him to. Expecting the curve, I was hit square in the chest with the pitch. The runner advanced and wound up scoring.

When the inning was over, I was still trying to figure out what was going on, and of course Matt was livid. As soon as I got in the dugout and started taking off my equipment, he screamed, "What's going on with you!"

I chucked my shin guards at him, which was all over ESPN's *SportsCenter* that night.

Stan immediately jumped between us, grabbed Matt, said, "You have no idea what's going on here," and got him cooled down.

When he turned to talk with me, I told him to leave me alone and got ready to hit. I was last up that inning and of course had no business even being in the box. Joe Girardi was managing the Marlins at the time, and one of his hard-throwing young guys was firing bullets.

The first pitch hit the catcher's glove, and I thought, *I never even saw that.* Next pitch, same thing. *I'm going to have to swing really early.*

I tried to focus on the ball and react as the third one streaked past me, but it felt like trying to swing a palm tree through peanut butter. That pitch could have hit me in the face and I wouldn't have so much as flinched.

I trudged back to the dugout barely aware of the backup catcher on his way out to warm up Matt while I was supposed to be getting my gear on. I slid my bat back into the rack, cleats clacking around me as my teammates made their way back onto the field.

I dropped wearily to the bench and hung my head. Stan Conte sat next me. "All right," I whispered. "You win." He nodded to Manager Felipe Alou, and I was done.

I tell you my own story only as evidence of the value of this new approach to youth sports. If old-school, small-town, midwestern, even biblical values—the ones I had been raised on—didn't work for me into adulthood, I wouldn't dare wave the flag for them as some answer to the ills of modern society as we know it.

I can tell you what would have become of me had I been a product of the Me Generation, what my friend and mentor Mike Hansen calls the get-all-you-can-while-you-can-then-sit-on-your-can crowd. I've seen it over and over. Those limelight guys who let the world revolve around them flourish as long as their astounding talent keeps them first in the hearts of the fans, their teammates, their coaches, and the media.

When adversity comes—an injury like mine, or a scandal, anything that diminishes their ability to produce as they once did—they're suddenly yesterday's news. There's always a new star on the horizon ready to become the next craze. Is there anything sadder than a faded hero desperate to hang on and taste that fame and adoration once more?

Had they focused on character and on making others better, when their skills declined—as they always do—they wouldn't be pitied as faded relics. They would be revered, admired, praised, their memories cherished. And they would likely be welcomed to continue doing what they had always done, just in a new capacity, as a broadcaster, commentator, or coach.

I confess being old school didn't make my abrupt transition easy. But I was never a worshipped superstar who was now forgotten. I went from everyday starter, respected by teammates and peers as a no-nonsense competitor, to virtually an invalid almost overnight.

Then, after more than a year of frustration and fear, wondering whether I would become an invalid and have to depend on my family to even function, I finally resigned myself to the fact that returning to baseball was off the table. That was a painful surrender, as you can imagine. I carefully weighed my options, considering what I could possibly do with the skill sets I had now.

My vision had been affected, my memory, my cognitive skills, even my ability to communicate. I had trouble finding the right words in normal conversations, once telling Steve Perry (famous lead singer of the rock band Journey), who said it was nice to meet me, that "it was nice to marry you." I was so humiliated, I wanted to just stay home with my family.

What can a man do who can't see, can't think, can't remember?

My only option was to become an umpire.

All right, that was uncalled for. Men in Blue, don't make my team pay for that lame attempt at humor.

In the long, horrible year since I had taken myself out of that last ball game, after enduring what seemed like endless tests and countless dizzy spells, three times driving away from the gas station with the hose still in my gas tank, and even getting lost running errands, at times I finally felt things were coming more clearly to me. I began to feel a little more comfortable in conversations. I was able to climb stairs without having to stop halfway up to let the sparkles fade or grab the railing till my dizziness subsided.

As I shared that good news with my doctor, Micky Collins, he urged me to still take it easy for another six months, reminding me that the brain is fragile and needs time to really heal. By then I wasn't about to do anything that would jeopardize my health. Every day I saw small, encouraging signs, and I was eager to let them build. When I compared how I felt to where I had been a year and more before that, I allowed myself to become optimistic.

I can't pinpoint the day I felt fully back to my old self, but I can tell you that as long as I live I never again want to endure what I went through. This had gone way beyond everything I knew about being a tough guy and playing through the daily aches and pains. I went from being the blind, stupid defender of the macho style of defending the plate at all costs to fully supporting the rule change that makes so much sense to Major League Baseball today. There's honor in soldiering on when you feel like giving up and giving in. Then there's the wisdom to know when your health and very life are at stake.

College kids and young professionals don't dare tell the truth and risk their scholarships or contracts. Kids in youth sports think they're invincible, don't want to be accused of being cowards, and don't recognize when they could have been seriously hurt. It falls to us adults to do the right thing, to stand in the gap, and to do everything in our power to guarantee that nothing close to what happened to me—and so many others—ever happens to a player who has been entrusted to us.

14

Seek Help When You Need It, Express Thanks When You Get It

KEY #8: HUMILITY

When I finally, reluctantly, gave up baseball, I missed a lot about the game: playing, competing, just *being* a ballplayer, being part of a team. But now that I could be out and about without wondering where I was or what I was doing or being afraid I'd drive off with the fuel nozzle still in my gas tank, I was able to get back into the sport in different capacities. I helped with one of my son's school teams. I did a little TV work. And the Cardinals brought me on as a part-time roving instructor, so I got to visit their teams throughout the organization. I found I had a knack for encouraging young players and enjoyed helping them improve.

For some reason, I also felt compelled to start studying the concept of servant leadership. If ever there was an example of a dichotomy, that's one. The normal question is "What are you, a servant or a leader?" But the point of servant leadership is leading by serving. It goes against everything we've ever been taught: There are leaders and there are followers, so lead, follow, or get out of the way, right?

I don't know if it was because of the influence of my dad, who had always been a quiet example of servant leadership, or of many of my coaches, who had also been proponents of that style.

Maybe I had picked it up from being raised in church and knowing that Jesus Himself had said that "he who is greatest among you shall be your servant. And whoever exalts himself will be humbled, and he who humbles himself will be exalted" (Matthew 23:11–13).

Whatever the reason, this "upside-down organizational chart" concept intrigued me, and I decided that whatever career path I chose for the next season of my life would somehow include it. The leader, the boss, puts himself at the bottom, in a supporting role, and empowers his subordinates to excel. Somehow, he loses no power or authority or respect. In fact, his stature is enhanced because he has honored the people entrusted to him.

Eager to start building a new life, I also involved myself in some business ventures, specifically real estate investments. Not being a fortune-teller, I did this at the worst possible time in my generation's history and wound up hurt badly by the economic downturn. Toughest was that my partners and I enjoyed some success just before the crash and so had optimistically extended ourselves. The resulting disaster was bad enough that my financial woes became news in the St. Louis area and, besides embarrassing me, effectively cured me of thinking I had found a new career path.

Needing help like never before, I reached out to eight trusted men and asked if they would come alongside, counsel me, and hold me accountable. I was amazed at how they rolled up their sleeves.

These eight I now lovingly refer to as my personal board are mostly business leaders (one is in ministry), and all have huge hearts. They are leaders in their respective fields and follow the servant leadership model I had been studying. With no personal agenda, they just wanted to help a friend out of a tough spot. At this critical crossroads in my life, these men became tireless mentors.

Over the years I had become aware that sometimes people enjoyed getting to know me mostly because I was a pro ballplayer. I tried to be discerning, but sometimes you can't be absolutely sure who your genuine friends are until you're in trouble. Some I thought were close were suddenly nowhere to be found when I no longer wore the uniform, especially when I fell into financial misfortune and it seemed the whole world knew about it.

You know where this story goes. It wouldn't be long before my fortunes reversed and my public profile became more positive than ever—something neither my board nor I had any inkling of when I went to them for help.

As you might imagine, suddenly I again had all the friends I needed. But by then I knew who my real friends were: the ones who were there for me when I had literally nothing to give back.

Few people are blessed with friends that true.

(I still make sure we get together as often as possible. I bring them to spring training, and I try to get each of them to join me on the road sometime during the season, if they can get away. They remain my financial accountability partners, and I bounce big decisions off them, depending on their areas of expertise. I also ask them to challenge me on leadership and recommend books and seminars I should be aware of, and I do the same for them.)

RIGHT AROUND THE time my board was helping me rebuild my finances, I responded to those parents' request that I coach the youth baseball team. Two years later a lot of water had passed under the bridge.

For a year I had been working with G.O. Ministries, Inc., a nonprofit short-term missions organization, planning a huge trip to the Dominican Republic with fifty kids and parents, including Kristin and three of our own. We would leave on a Saturday, work our tails off on service projects, play doubleheaders against local kids every day until Thursday, meet up with Albert Pujols and his wife in an impoverished village where his foundation had built a ball field, play an all-star team there, then take a day off, and fly home seven days after we had gotten there.

I couldn't wait. Some local businessmen, former athletes themselves who liked how we were doing things, stepped up big and financed the trip for all the boys. It would be the experience of a lifetime for most of these kids. We'd been teaching them servanthood stateside, but they had never seen poverty like they would in the DR. Plus it would be fun to show them how their hero, Albert, was worshipped down there and what he had done for the people of his homeland.

The Wednesday before we were to leave I flew to Bristol, Connecticut, to announce the American and National League Gold Glove–winning pitchers and catchers on ESPN. Right in the middle of my live broadcast, my cell phone vibrated in my back pocket, almost making me lose my train of thought. When my segment ended and I sat offstage watching the next one, I checked my phone. The screen read, "Missed call, John Mozeliak."

Mo is general manager of the Cardinals, who had won the World Series a few weeks before. Just then a text popped up. "Need you in the office 10 a.m. Friday to interview for the manager's job."

I sat staring at the screen. *Are you kidding me?*

Tony La Russa had recently resigned after sixteen incredible years, so everybody knew the Cardinals were looking. Names of candidates had been floating around in the press, but mine had certainly not been one of them.

Interview? Uh-oh. I've never had a job interview in my life.

Trying to keep my hands from shaking, I immediately texted the news to my board and added, "I need a crash course. By the time I get back tomorrow morning, if you could send me some of the toughest questions you've ever used when interviewing someone for a top leadership position, I'd really appreciate it."

This was their world, and they immediately began sending some of the best material I could have asked for. Most people with their eye on a coveted position spend years climbing the corporate ladder to position themselves for the best advantage. All I could do in fewer than thirty-six hours was virtually submit myself to these guys.

They did a fantastic job preparing me. They even advised me what color suit and tie to wear; then they outlined the topics the brass would likely want to talk about—things a baseball player would never think of. They had me thinking at a whole new level. They grilled me on the subject of leadership and predicted that one of the key open-ended questions would be what I thought the job should look like.

By Friday morning, it was all over the news that the Cardinals were talking with five candidates. The other four were:

- Terry Francona, who had managed both the Phillies and the Red Sox, winning two World Series with Boston (now manager of the Cleveland Indians)
- Chris Maloney, for five years the manager of the Cardinals' AAA Memphis Redbirds (now our first-base coach)
- Joe McEwing, former AAA manager in the White Sox organization and now White Sox third-base coach
- José Oquendo, a former popular utility player for the Cardinals and since 2000 their third-base coach (now our third-base coach and infielders coach)

I was clearly the least experienced, and had you asked me if I thought I would be chosen, I probably would have said no. But what an honor to even be considered! I had played five seasons for the Cardinals several years before and was now a roving instructor, yet they saw something that made them want to interview me. That alone was a huge compliment.

I sincerely believed I had nothing to lose, and I felt so prepared that I headed to owner Bill DeWitt's office at the stadium with an overwhelming sense of peace. One thing I knew for sure: I wanted the job. All I could do was be myself and not pretend to be something I wasn't or apologize for my lack of experience. The Cardinals knew who I was. I hadn't applied for this position. I did have a sense of the organization, having visited all the ball clubs and seen a lot of their young talent.

And of course my board had been right. After a few pleasantries, the first question was what I thought the job was about.

I said, "You know, I think it's about more than baseball. I
think it's about leadership."

The interview lasted three hours, but the time flew by. While
we covered the expected baseball strategy and game situations, I
really enjoyed discussing servant leadership and what that could
mean to a team.

When they raised issues I was unsure of, I said I hoped to
surround myself with people who had expertise in those areas,
because my goal would be to give the players the best opportunity to succeed.

In the end, I couldn't think of a question I hadn't been prepared for.

As the meeting concluded, management mentioned that they
had already interviewed a couple of the other candidates, had a
few more to talk to, and that they would get back to me "one way
or the other" within a few days. When I told them I was leaving
the next morning for a week in the Dominican Republic, they
told me to stay accessible and someone would call me Thursday.

I felt I had done everything I could do, and I had no regrets.
I walked out, silently thanking God for the opportunity and for
having had clear thoughts and being able to communicate what
I believed I could bring to the table.

THE TRIP FELL at the right time, because I would be out of the
country when my phone started ringing over the news that I had
become part of the manager search, giving me the perfect excuse
not to answer.

We had been working a long time to provide this experience

for the boys, and I didn't want to shortchange them. I had spent the last two years with them, but when I got to the airport Saturday morning, they all looked at me like I was a different person. They peppered me with questions, but I nipped that in the bud, telling them I didn't know any more than they did and that there was nothing to talk about yet.

Once we got to the DR, there was no time to be distracted by anything else. The kids were stunned by the great need, got to work, and stayed busy. In the mornings, some of us used sledgehammers and crowbars to help tear down buildings to make room for charity medical clinics, while others dug ditches for sewer lines. The kids worked like never before.

We'd go straight from there to some of the worst areas and feed poor kids the only meal they'd get that day. The boys were in charge of delivering food to the kids and then cleaning up afterward. During the meal they sat with kids from these shantytowns and figured out a way to communicate, despite the language barrier. Many of the kids they were feeding were their own age, and the contrast in lifestyle hit them right between the eyes.

Exhausted from a full morning's work, the boys went back to the G.O. ministry house to change into their uniforms. We had been assigned to two 20-by-20 cinder-block rooms, one for the men and boys and the other for the ladies and girls. These were jammed wall to wall with triple bunk beds. The facility was clean and safe, but many creature comforts—like being able to flush the toilet paper—were gone, and that was perfect. We weren't there to be pampered. Our boys, my own included, were exposed to a life they had never seen before.

Then we had to chase goats out of a field so we could play the local kids in a doubleheader. People sat atop the dugouts and in the trees watching the American kids play.

Lying in my bunk at the end of a long day in the oppressive heat, it would hit me and I would have to chuckle. *I'm still in the mix to become manager of the Cardinals.*

Some of the parents were well connected in the St. Louis corporate world and would occasionally pull me aside and tell me their e-mails were saying it looked like I had a chance. I'd say, "Hey, if it happens, it happens, but I haven't heard a thing yet."

The most I would allow myself to dream was that maybe my having been interviewed would open the door to a look from other organizations, or maybe the Cardinals would ask me to manage one of their minor-league teams. Kristin and I had to think about whether we were prepared for that, having me away from home for the better part of a year for who knew how long?

This whole idea hadn't even been on my radar a few days before, and within a week of receiving that late-night text, I would know "one way or the other" about my future.

Thursday our dog-tired band of social workers rolled into Batey Aleman, where Albert and Deidre Pujols's foundation had built a field, bought uniforms, and run clinics for the local kids in past years. Now he had arranged for our boys to play them, and he turned it into a huge deal.

Our team thought we were just going to play a game, but we were greeted by kids with trumpets who led us on a parade through the shanty shacks of Batey Aleman, really more of a refugee camp than a town. The whole ceremony, including a presentation and welcoming celebration, lasted ninety minutes in the smoking sun.

On top of that, their talented ballplayers beat us in front of a raucous home crowd that really pulled for their team. Our kids did well against the hardest-throwing pitcher they had ever faced, and by the end of it, we were spent. Fortunately, we would have a day and a half to decompress before flying home.

Albert had brought in a cook and erected a huge tent where he fed the other team and most of the people in that village. Then he fed our whole group a wonderful chicken and rice meal. He and his wife had to catch a flight to Miami, where he was being courted by the Marlins now that he was a free agent (he would, of course, wind up with the Angels). Before they left, I thanked him for the fantastic job he had done hosting us, and he congratulated me on being interviewed by the Cardinals. Having been his friend as long as I had, I could tell he thought that was probably the extent of it.

Just as I returned to the table next to Kristin, my phone buzzed and the screen read, "John Mozeliak." When I excused myself to take it, I felt all the kids' eyes on me.

I said, "John, give me a second to get to where I can talk. . . ."

I hurried behind a brightly painted shack where they were cooking, but everybody was still watching, so I moved farther around the side.

Mo said, "Mike, I just want to say congratulations. You're going to be the next manager of the St. Louis Cardinals. . . ."

I froze.

"But you've got to do me a favor. You can't tell anybody. We're not announcing it until Sunday. Will you be back in town?"

I told him we'd be back Saturday. "Can I tell my wife?"

"Yes, but make sure it doesn't get out before we announce it."

When I returned to the table, I felt fifty pairs of eyes on me, and I realized that literally seconds after getting the job I was facing my first test. Could I be trusted to keep my word?

I sat and I waited for the awkwardness to subside, then started eating again as if nothing had happened. With my phone in my lap I texted, "I got the job, but don't react because we can't say anything till Sunday" and tapped Kristin's leg with it.

She casually looked at it under the table and just kept eating, and I thought, *Well, you could have reacted a little to me!* Here I had just landed the job of a lifetime, and no response from my wife. But it was my own fault. She was only doing what I'd asked. I couldn't believe her game face with all those eyes on us. When we got time later to talk about it, we couldn't help but shake our heads and laugh.

That night we held a ceremony where each boy told the group what he had seen, what he had learned, and what had impressed him the most during the week. I was so proud of how the boys stood before the others and shared. More important, I could see they had truly been touched by what they had experienced and understood the importance of the difference they could make in the world.

When I wrapped things up, I had a hard time keeping my emotions together, thrilled about my new job but knowing it would take me away from all this. I think many of the boys realized something was up, but I didn't even tell my own sons.

I finally texted all five kids as I was walking into the press conference that Sunday, about three minutes before the Cardinals introduced me as their new manager.

Second only to sharing that thrill with Kristin and the kids was the joy of calling each of the men on my board to thank them individually for the role they had played in helping me get the job. I try to touch base with each of them at least once a month, and every time I do, I am challenged, encouraged, and better for it.

Naturally the early public debate about me, at the time the youngest manager in the big leagues and the least experienced, was the colossal contrast between me and the legend I was replacing.

Tony La Russa was headed for the Hall of Fame. To many, I was Mike Who?

Some speculated that I was the transition guy, the one who would take all the heat during the inevitable collapse between the glory years and when another marquee manager would be hired.

Others said I was a budget move, the one the Cardinals could justify paying the least.

Still others said I was in a no-win situation. If the team did well, it was because anyone could succeed if they had inherited the defending World Series champions built by my predecessor. And if the team failed, what did anyone expect from an unqualified manager?

I just wanted a chance to do the job. And I confess I privately resented the idea that I was underqualified. No one could deny my lack of experience, but saying the organization had chosen an unqualified manager—for whatever reason—was an insult to them. They might have been wrong about me; that would have to be determined by how the team did under my leadership.

But I did not like being constantly referred to as the guy who jumped directly from coaching youth league to managing in the big leagues—true or not.

But then, when the Cardinals started to do okay and it looked like I wasn't getting in their way, I began to embrace that angle and play to it myself. I'd say, "I can't explain our success. What do I know? I'm brand new at this."

It also gave me credibility when I spoke about dreaming and reaching for the stars. I could say, "Last year I was coaching kids. Next thing you know, I'm managing a team that won the World Series last year. Go figure."

The
Manifesto Impact

Though it really wasn't that long ago, much has happened since I endured the uncomfortable silence of my own living room, reading that letter to fellow parents.

It seemed such a good idea at the time. But hearing only the gentle crackling in the fireplace behind me and my own voice—less confident with every sentence—I wondered why I hadn't realized how long it would take to read five single-spaced pages. Even editing myself on the fly, it seemed to go on and on.

I still remember peeking up for a hint of moral support and finding the eyes of only John Mabry, the one person in the room besides Kristin who had seen the document in advance. He sat next to his wife, Ann, with a raised-brow, told-you-so look. Thanks, John.

Well, at least the rest of the parents knew what they would be getting into if they really wanted me to coach that team. Now was the time to pull the plug, if that was their decision.

The fact was, I wanted the job. I was excited about the possibilities. I closed with "I'm not guaranteeing this is what's going to happen to our boys, but I want you to see that this system works."

I said that not just because the small-town team I had played for back in Ohio from age ten through seventeen produced five professionals, including a big leaguer—not to mention dozens of college players. The much larger issue concerned the majority of kids who progressed through such a system and never played organized sports again. But they grew together and learned lessons that lasted far beyond their baseball experience.

Those fellow parents overlooked my clumsy approach, forgave my insensitivity, and set aside their misgivings long enough to take a chance and entrust me with their kids. Despite fits and starts and lessons learned the hard way, we can now say our experiment was a success.

In my role as manager of the Cardinals, I don't have lofty ideas about how many championships I have to win. My job is to show leadership and impact people. That's what we were trying to accomplish with the youth-league team, and now I'm applying that same approach in a big-league clubhouse. I've gone from the reluctant voice of a new approach to the public face for a letter I would never have labeled a manifesto, but which has taken on a life of its own.

I was honored to be a coach, and now I'm humbled to be a manager and hopefully a mentor. My goal, my obligation, is to pass along what has been imparted to me. When I get that right and serve my guys without any other agenda or motive or need to be acknowledged for it, I win their trust and know I have done my job.

That's what I meant from the beginning when I said youth sports had to be all about the kids.

Now, I have a new perspective after helping a generation of young people fall in love with the game, get their opportunities to shine, and above all become people of character, regardless the level of athletic achievement they reach.

It's fun to win, and at the big-league level, that's how most people define success. But if our grand experiment proved valid, it ought to work as well for adults as kids. I'm living proof that it does, because I get my greatest joy as a manager when I make a move because of what only I know is going on with one of my players. Maybe something makes him physically or emotionally unable to do what he needs to do, so I find a way around it. He's protected, I own the decision, and I'm the one who gets beat up over it by the media and the public.

The guy in question knows I took a bullet for him, and that's all that matters. When broadcasters, writers, or fans demand to know how I could make such a move—playing someone I seemingly shouldn't or not playing someone I seemingly should—I could defend myself and make myself look good. But the honorable thing is to remind myself why I am where I am—to do the right thing because it's the right thing, as we tried to teach the youth-team kids every day.

What's next? None of us can know for certain. But I love this game, and every day I wake up praying it doesn't rain, because that gives me one more chance to (1) teach someone to play the right way, (2) have a positive impact on them, and (3) do it with class.

All I want to do is keep learning and growing and helping others do the same.

AFTERWORD

by Bob Costas

October 16, 2014
Game 5, National League Championship Series

Amid the delirium at AT&T Park, following Travis Ishikawa's dramatic home run to win the pennant for the Giants, and end the Cardinals' season—a smaller, barely noted scene stood out for me. As his disappointed players trudged toward their clubhouse, Mike Matheny waited at the dugout railing. Waited until he could make eye contact with Giants manager, Bruce Bochy. Then, in a brief and understated moment, he lifted his cap and nodded toward his victorious counterpart. A small gesture perhaps, but one that tells you a lot about Mike Matheny.

You win, or in this case, lose, with class. With integrity. You play hard. You play smart. You respect yourself, your teammates, your opponents, and your craft. It's a game and it should be fun. It's a business, and those realities are there, too. But it can be more than just that. It can, at least for some, be an expression of principles. Many of the same principles Mike Matheny first spelled out in his letter to the parents of young baseball players he coached, far from the spotlight of the big leagues.

In many ways, Matheny's still new, but already extremely successful, tenure with the Cardinals is an ongoing example of those principles writ large.

ABOUT THE AUTHORS

MIKE MATHENY played thirteen years as a catcher for four major-league teams, won four Gold Gloves, and holds the MLB record for most consecutive games without an error; 2015 will mark his fourth year as manager of the St. Louis Cardinals. Matheny led the Cardinals to the postseason in each of his first three campaigns, winning the National League pennant in 2013. He and his wife, Kristin, are the parents of five and live in St. Louis. For more information about Mike's Catch 22 Foundation and to keep up with his blog, visit www.MikeMatheny.com.

JERRY B. JENKINS is the author of twenty *New York Times* bestsellers, including the Left Behind series. His writing has appeared in *Time, Reader's Digest, Parade, Guideposts,* and dozens of Christian periodicals. He has collaborated on as-told-to autobiographies by Hank Aaron, Orel Hershiser, Walter Payton, Nolan Ryan, Mike Singletary, and Billy Graham. For more information about Jerry, visit www.JerryJenkins.com.

DATE DUE

OCT 1 6 2015		
FEB 1 2 2016		
DEC 1 2 2016		

DEMCO 38-296